Music of Pure Love

Music of Pure Love:

Where Angels Gladly Tread

by
Thomas G. Casey, S.J.

Templegate Publishers
Springfield, Illinois

First published in 2006 by
Templegate Publishers, LLC
302 East Adams Street
P.O. Box 5152
Springfield, Illinois 62705-5152
217-522-3353
templegate.com

ISBN 10: 0-87243-271-8
ISBN 13: 978-0-87243-271-0
Library of Congress Control Number
2006909049

De licentia superiorum ordinis

Cover: William Blake's *Jacob's Ladder*

To my niece Rebecca:
as you set out on the journey of life,
may you believe in God's immense love for you
at every step.

Whatever is true, whatever is noble, whatever is right, whatever is pure, whatever is lovely, whatever is admirable, if anything is excellent and praiseworthy, fill your mind with these things.

Saint Paul, Letter to the Philippians 4:8

Unless you can love, as the angels may,
With the breadth of heaven betwixt you;
Unless you can dream that his faith is fast,
Through behoving and unbehoving:
Unless you can die when the dream is past —
Oh, never call it loving!

Elizabeth Barrett Browning, "A Woman's Shortcomings"

Contents

Prologue

Tuning to a New Frequency

For I am convinced that neither death nor life, neither angels nor demons, neither the present nor the future, nor any powers, neither height nor depth, nor anything else in creation, will be able to separate us from the love of God that is in Christ Jesus our Lord.

Saint Paul, Letter to the Romans 8:38-39

Let us fly toward our beloved fatherland . . . For we have a fatherland from which we come and a Father who waits for us there.

Plotinus, *Enneads* I, 6, 8.

As Jesus was suffering the anguish of abandonment in the Garden of Gethsemane the night before he was crucified, an angel was sent from heaven to comfort him. This heavenly messenger was on one of the most delicate assignments ever — he was sent by the Father to console his only Son. How do you comfort the Son of God when he is shedding drops of blood in perspiration? How do you give companionship to one whose three closest friends are fast asleep and who knows another friend is on his way to betray him? How do you slake the thirst of God's Son when he can only taste the bitterness of a bottomless cup of suffering?

The angel of comfort knew exactly what to do, for even though he was in an earthly garden next to Jesus, he was also perennially present before the throne of God in paradise. The Father had sent his Son into the world as Savior and Redeemer and in the deep darkness of that moment the angel shone a light showing face after face of the saved and redeemed — women and men, black and white, young and old, rich and poor. They extended right through history, from Adam and Eve to the last couple in the world; they came from innumerable cultures — high-density urban landscapes and trackless wastes in remote corners of the globe. They sat at the sick beds of friends and listened patiently to their catalog of miseries; they lingered long before the tombstones of loved ones, entrusting them to God's mercy; they taught in schools and universities with love and dedication; they knelt before the tabernacle in countryside chapels; they wholeheartedly forgave those who offended them. And each apparition was like a welcome transfusion of blood into the suffering heart of Jesus. The sight of these wonders of his love sent new strength coursing through his veins.

Even if everything turned dark, and the world became utterly depraved, God's infinite love is so unimaginably vast and creative that good is bound to triumph, we know not how. We ought never lose hope. In fact the worse evil becomes, the more majestically God's love will rise in our midst. He will grace us with something great, a resurrection.

As the French Jesuit priest and mystic Marie Joseph Pierre Teilhard de Chardin (1881-1955) so eloquently expressed it:

> Someday, after mastering the winds, the waves, the tides and gravity, we shall harness for God the energies of love, and then, for a second time in the history of the world, the human being will have discovered fire.

As the small story of a personal life unfolds, it seems that each year runs by more quickly than the last. We witness the same pattern in the large story that is history. The pace of change increased dramatically in the twentieth century; now it is hyper-accelerating. The potency of computer chips is multiplying at an exponential rate. Technology powers civilization forward at such a dizzying speed that we are not sure where the ride is taking us and whether we will be happy with the destination. Spiritual change, whether for good or bad, is also accelerating. Some people are choosing God with such an intense love that they are becoming angelic. Others give themselves freely into slavery to sin and descend into abysmal depths. The majority are in between — although their love does not shine forth like the saints, the goodness of grace is quietly at work in their lives.

A time is dawning (how near to us we do not know) when the world will be blessed with women and men as great and inspirational as the saints of the first centuries of Christianity. Ancient pagan Rome was soaked with their blood, which is why it became Christian. The remains of many of these martyrs are threaded throughout the city like a hidden rosary of the glorious mysteries. Beneath the ornate splendor of the Eternal City and the distracting noise of its incessant traffic, the martyrs are embedded in the silent layers of its soil. They are the real treasures of Rome, discreetly placed inside the big basilicas, sealed in subterranean crypts, lying in the underground labyrinth of catacombs beyond the ancient city walls, quiet and humble witnesses to the greatest love of all. Deeply rooted in God, the blood of the martyrs gave supernatural life to the ancient church, helping it to blossom despite intense persecution. The stifling world climate that is gathering today seems hostile to Christianity in a more insidious manner. Because the cultural winds swirling around are so disorienting, the great saints of this new era will be profoundly rooted in Christ so as not to be blown away. During historical periods when whole cultures supported the choice to be a disciple of Christ, Christians were partially carried in God's direction by the prevailing wind. That tailwind can no longer be counted on. Yet despite the adverse spiritual weather, the new giants of goodness will truly be salt of the earth, through being grounded in Christ. Just as a pinch of salt can enhance the flavor of food, so they shall have a worldwide impact that far exceeds their numbers. Like salt they will function as an antiseptic, destroying the germs of evil, and have a cleansing effect, bringing purity. They will counteract spiritual disintegration, and with God's grace revive goodness in an unexpected and breathtaking way.

There are extraordinary pockets of goodness in our world. There are decent and upright people like Abel and Noah, but there is also murder and corruption to rival Cain and the later times of the Flood, except in our era we have had the benefit of Christ and two thousand years of Christianity, which they had not. Nonetheless angelic success is possible:

Christians who will become saints in this new era that is dawning will fix their spiritual gaze upon God, wed their interests to his in a nuptial embrace, and seek his glory everywhere and at every moment, a glory which is also the glory of each believer. This success will be achieved by choosing love over hatred. Love excels any other power in the universe; it even defeats hell.

Pure love raises us to the exquisite pitch of God. If you take your place in an auditorium a short time before a concert begins, you notice the various musicians tuning their instruments. As each musician makes the necessary adjustments, the orchestra begins to emit a distinctly odd sound. It is as though each instrument were singing a language of its own, inhabiting a separate world, and during this time there are more than a few "false starts" as each musician endeavors to arrive at the right pitch. These moments that precede the concert are like birth-pangs, the sometimes painful and painfully sounding efforts to enter into something larger than any one instrumentalist could produce. In this book I am trying to tune up as well to something which escapes categorization and cannot be tidily or neatly summed up in words. It is a mystery that needs to be approached a number of times, using different instruments in order to get the pitch right. And I hope that what I say at times shows the inspiration of the One who is the source of harmony, who orchestrated a beautiful order from primal chaos, hovering in rhythmical perfection over the waters at the beginning of creation, regular and reassuring as the sound of a mother's heartbeat heard across the internal sea that encircles the womb.

I hope that the humming of music can be heard underneath the words of this book. I devote an entire chapter to

13

the opera *Don Giovanni*, one of the masterpieces of arguably the most brilliant composer ever, Wolfgang Amadeus Mozart, of whom someone said that his music was so beautiful it could entice even angels to earth. I dedicate another chapter to the patron saint of music, the early Christian martyr Cecilia. There is something loosely musical about this book. Each chapter returns again to pure love, like musical variations on a single theme. What I am trying to approach is beyond words. It is celebrated in the songs of angels. Pure love is a song of rejoicing. It is a song that fully claims the human being. It gathers the dissonant fragments of life into a beautiful melody. The notes of this melody are rich and full, and they are all in the key of love. It is not a song that must be deferred until paradise; it is not a hymn that only angels can sing. This special song is open to all and can be sung by each in a unique manner.

This book is an invitation to sing a new song, and embark upon a journey that will shape character in a new way through an ancient vision. It offers to unleash the limitless potential with which we are graced. This guide is clear enough to illuminate the way, flexible enough to be adapted in diverse ways and solid enough to last the course. This program is not complicated to understand, but courage and boldness are necessary to put it into practice. Although there is much practical advice in this book, it is concerned above all with seeing ourselves and our world in a new way. This new vision unfolds in the light. The darkness that likes to lay siege to our souls must be firmly refused and forcefully rejected; the light is more than ready to embrace us.

How can we arrive at purity of love, something that of its nature we associate with people whose goodness is angelic? I am not going to map out a 10 week course or a

20 point program. Instead I am going to use stories interspersed with moments of reflection. A story is a surer and quicker way to the heart than the best designed program. I will not tell tall tales but real stories that are moving and portray the purity of love as something attractive and more than worthwhile. There are more than enough false stories circulating in our culture: beautifully-crafted novels and films which enter our emotional world and touch our sensibilities only to coax us into condoning and sympathizing with actions that we know in our more lucid moments to be wrong. Both movies and books can all too easily present happenings such as a man making love with women other than his wife in terms of the man's quest for fulfillment, rather than as the cruel destruction of his wife's life and the careless killing of his own soul.

Novels are for reading and films for seeing; celluloid and fictional stories do not present themselves in the form of arguments, so viewers and readers are not given the opportunity to disagree with them. Despite the falsehood that is intertwined with their truth, these stories are not aimed primarily at the rational mind; instead they sway the emotions and sweep them along, making an informed and critical response less likely. This book is full of stories of a different kind: not stories that manipulate emotions, but ones that speak simply and without artifice of the greatest values on earth, the ones that provide a sure path to paradise. I will not try to impose these stories; I will offer them with great respect for the precious gift of human freedom.

If we want to find pure love, we need to find God because if God does not live in us as a welcome guest, we cannot have the purity of love. Angels are pure because they are permanently and powerfully in God's presence. If they lost God, purity would desert them as well. How can we tune into God's wavelength in the perfect and continual manner that angels do? Obviously we cannot become disincarnate spirits. There is no way we can imitate angels by casting our bodies aside and deluding ourselves that we are not bound by the material world. As the witty and incisive French essayist Michel de Montaigne (1533-1592) commented: "even on the most exalted throne in the world, we are still only sitting on our own posterior." Yet we are often tempted to betray our human nature in the illusory belief that we can thereby deify ourselves. It is the oldest temptation of all: "you will be like God," the serpent slyly insinuates to Eve (Genesis 3:5). But trying to be an angel or a god ends up having an undesired effect: "the human being is neither an angel nor a beast, and the misfortune is that the one who would act the angel acts the beast." (Blaise Pascal, 1623-1662)

Nevertheless there is a real and promising way in which we can imitate angels: by dedicating ourselves wholly to God, by approaching God with reverential confidence; by longing for and loving everything that speaks to us of God; by loving him in everything we do. The most practical self-measurement of our love for God and others is to ask ourselves at each moment whether the action we are doing or about to do is one which Jesus would do in the same way in our place. Would Jesus think these thoughts? Would he speak this way? Would he love people like this? If we can answer an honest yes to each of these questions, then one day at the end of time the Father will answer a huge yes when the Son asks him if he recognizes us as his children. But we won't be able to answer these questions unless we get to know how Jesus thinks and speaks and acts through reading the Gospels and spending time with him in the interior conversation of prayer. There has never been a saint who did not pray. Meeting God does not demand geographical displacement because he already dwells within us. Millions of people are unaware of this. Like the protagonist of James Joyce's autobiographical novel *A Portrait of the Artist as a Young Man*, they consider him in the fashion of an absentee landlord who is uncaring and self-engrossed: "The artist, like the God of creation, remains within or behind or beyond or above his handiwork, invisible, refined out of existence, indifferent, paring his fingernails." This view of Joyce's Stephen Dedalus is not only untrue, but in certain essential ways the reverse of the truth. God is not indifferent, for no one cares for us more than he does. No one else can be nearer to us and more intimate with us than God. As Saint Augustine realized, God is closer to us than we are to ourselves.

Isn't it all too simple — thinking, speaking, and acting like Jesus, loving God in everything we do, praying and reading scripture? Isn't there something more? There is and there isn't. There is — because what you are reading is only the introduction to the book and pure love is such an awesome mystery that it can be illuminated in billions of different ways while still remaining a mystery. There isn't — because although I am approaching the music of pure love in a new way, it is still the same unmistakable and timeless song. With this book I am confirming an age-old tradition even as I launch a new beginning.

Can something so straightforward really work? Let me answer with a story. The Second Book of Kings tells the story of Naaman, the commander of the king's army in

17

Syria, a man of great valor, but afflicted with leprosy. Having no doubt consulted the best doctors in Syria to no avail, he travels to Israel in search of healing. The prophet Elisha hears of his plight and has Naaman sent to him. The commander arrives in splendid style, loaded down with gifts of gold, silver and clothing. But when he arrives at Elisha's door, the prophet does not even bother to come out to meet him, but simply sends a messenger to tell him that if he wants to be healed, all he has to do is wash seven times in the River Jordan. Naaman is furious. He cannot believe that he has traveled all this distance to receive such a ridiculously simple suggestion. He cannot see what is so special about foreign water. He is convinced that the rivers of Damascus are much better. Used as he is to commanding respect, Naaman cannot endure being treated in such a dismissive way by a prophet who does not even deign to meet him face to face. Naaman probably feels he is being humiliated. He turns away in anger, but his own servants plead with him. "My father, if the prophet had told you to do some great thing, would you not have done it? How much more, then, when he tells you, 'Wash and be cleansed!'" (2 Kings 5:13). Naaman relents and follows the prophet's bidding. Not only does his skin become smooth and pure like a baby's, but he is also healed of his pride.

The astonishing miracle of being cleansed from the leprosy of evil, of finding our spiritual "skin" as pure and radiant as an innocent child, does not happen through spectacular events, but as a result of washing our most ordinary actions in the blood of Jesus, through uniting them with him. It is through dipping our thoughts, words, and actions into the purifying river of his blood that we are healed and made pure: ". . . we have confidence to enter the Most Holy Place by the blood of Jesus" (Hebrews 10:19).

This continual awareness of Jesus demands vigilance and effort, yet it brings great joy equanimity. It is the ultimate diet: fasting from hatred, anger, strife, and all the other evils that tear us apart. It is about purifying our lives. It is not a diet that battles against fat or physical unattractiveness. Here the stakes are much higher. The focus is not on losing weight, but on winning love.

In the Beatitudes, Jesus blesses the pure of heart. The pure of heart are angelic because every beat of their heart is for God. They are focused totally on God. Pure people constantly think of God and talk to him again and again as they would to a best friend. They remember the sufferings of Jesus and try to console him through their compassion and gratitude. They identify with God's interests and priorities and actively seek to bring them about. They are so convinced of the excellence of God's cause that they do not shirk at suffering for it. They do not want to be influenced by anything or anyone other than God. The pure of heart love with a gratuitous and selfless love, refusing to mix love with utilitarian considerations. Their love is just that — love. I have been lucky to meet people like this. Although their purity will never be featured on the cover of celebrity magazines, their goodness leaves behind a fragrance that is unforgettable. Their hearts are so ablaze with the love of God that anyone who comes near them cannot help but feel a delightful and mysterious warmth.

Such purity seems beyond anything we could ever reach. Our own petty goodness is miserly by comparison. Could we ever become pure ourselves? We can draw courage from the example of people unimaginably far from

19

God who have become immeasurably pure after embracing the message of Christ. Just as they once gave themselves completely to evil, so they come to surrender totally to God. Like Saint Paul, one of the bitterest enemies of Christ and Christianity, who was to become the greatest missionary of the early Church, their loyalties are absolute. Persons like these concretely incarnate God's commandment to love with all their heart and soul and mind and strength. They refuse to settle for mediocrity. They tirelessly strive to become better. They are not satisfied with even the least blemish. Although they know that God's love cancels out their past, they nevertheless put all their energy into making up for the wasted years. But their remembrance of the past never causes despair since the memory is submerged in an ocean of trust and gratitude at God's mercy. The example of extremely bad people who reach unexpected heights of goodness is a living demonstration of the fact that however horrendous the evil we have committed, it cannot prevent us from becoming outstanding in goodness with God's help.

However, Rome was not built in a day, and purity of heart does not happen instantly. We are creatures of flesh and blood, and our weaknesses often get the better of us. We should not be shocked when we make mistakes. Certainly we should be sorry for grieving God, though with a peaceful sorrow, soothed by humility and trust. With confidence in God, we can easily recover our serenity when we fall, because we believe that God is merciful and despite our failures will help us even more in the future. With humility, we are not surprised at our own lack of love, for we do not confuse ourselves with God.

While not being taken aback by our mistakes, we should not become complacent about them, resigning ourselves to living relatively upright but ungenerous lives. It would be a tragedy not to seize the day, not to live each passing moment in its fullness, not to attempt great things for God's glory. It would be heartbreaking to stand before God at the Last Judgment and hear his sad words, "you desired so little, you were content with mere scraps, you suffered from permanent spiritual malnutrition when you could have really *lived*." A life of small misdemeanors and tiny failings that are hardly noticed and never regretted sooner or later has a cumulative effect: God is gradually but firmly ushered out. But a life fired by a noble purpose and consumed by a great goal is the one of the supreme beauties of the human spirit. This was the kind of life Saint Paul came to lead, straining forward to what lay ahead of him, pressing and pushing toward the goal, no longer living himself but opening his heart so much that Christ could now live in him.

If you are ready to be generous with your soul, or if you are even contemplating such readiness, this book could be for you. The story of this book culminates in a love song that relives the extraordinary wedding day of the patroness of music, the amazing young noblewoman from Rome, Saint Cecilia. Her superlative testimony is a crowning moment in the story of pure love. In this prologue I have already started searching for the right musical notes, like a musician of the spirit tuning to the pitch of purity. But finding the right pitch is not an automatic discovery, and in Chapter one I share my own experience of getting sidetracked on the journey and failing to pace myself to the rhythm of grace. As a teenager I imagined I could move from impurity to purity in a single magically mystical moment. I figured it would happen automatically once I crossed the threshold of a monastery; so I decided to leave the world and become a monk. Somehow I presumed that once I entered the cloister I would instantly slough off my humanity and become angelic. I did not realize that I was trying to leave reality behind for a world of fantasy.

Tuning to the wrong pitch of purity leads to the cacophony of frigidity and repression. Chapter two shows how this fallen frequency broadcasts lies about purity, and reveals nothing of its sheer abundance and lush life.

There is a phrase that has often bewildered tourists seeking road directions in Ireland: "If I were you, I wouldn't start from here at all." Life would be easier if the starting point on the road to pure love were not the impurity within which we find ourselves, but such a life would also be unreal. Chapter three insists on taking seriously our humble point of departure but also refuses to let it discourage us. With God's help, enormous progress is more than possible.

Chapter four envisions the quest for pure love as a strenuous yet blessed activity, as hard work carried by grace. Chapter five paints the big picture within which our lives unfold: the double movement of history, one tendency drawing everything upwards, the other attempting to drag everything down. And within this large-scale historical drama, each human being can realize the purest and noblest act that can rise from this world, by giving a full-blooded yes to God's invitation to be good.

Evil can turn up in the most alluring guises and Chapter six tells of a deceptive song that does not lead to pure love, yet repeatedly seduces people with its ambivalent beauty. Chapter seven provides concrete guidelines for harmonizing our song with God's chorus so that we can sing with confidence and success. Chapter eight continues to give practical advice on how to switch to the wavelength of fullness and love through following the voice of the Spirit. Chapter nine tells the heartening story of someone who found God's song that was also her own and sang it. I hope this book helps you sing your song. It would be a shame if you never did.

1

Mistaken Journey

In the beginning God created the heavens and the earth. Now the earth was formless and empty, darkness was over the surface of the deep, and the Spirit of God was hovering over the waters.

(Genesis 1:1-2)

Success is not final, failure is not fatal: it is the courage to continue that counts.

Winston Churchill

Matthew's Gospel tells us that after the birth of Jesus, the angel of the Lord appeared to Joseph in a dream, telling him to get up, take the child and his mother, and flee into Egypt and stay there until he was told otherwise, for King Herod was about to search for the child in order to kill it. As an idealistic adolescent I made a journey that my parents and family found as sudden and unexpected as Joseph and Mary must have found theirs — except in my case, I had not been listening to an angel, but to enchanting voices of my own making.

"I'm off now. I might never see you again, so good-bye." The words were uttered quickly, with an apologetic tone for having spoken in such eternal terms and for having expedited it so quickly.

I had been about to get into the car with my parents in order to leave the world behind: I was fleeing from the filthy lowlands of civilization; I wanted to breathe the pure air of the monastic heights. The billowing drama of this grand exit was punctured by my mother's reproachful reminder, "at least say goodbye to your brother".

For her, the fact that I had neglected this essential farewell cast a shameful shadow over the kind of leave I was taking. A leave of my senses, she fancied. I was 17 years of age, and had just completed secondary schooling and my final examination. I was about to set out on a short physical journey. I was drawn by the immense spiritual progress it promised. Neil Armstrong's famous words rang in my mind, 'that's one small step for man, one giant leap for mankind.' The only lunar connection my mother could see was in my *lunacy*.

The fact that I had not thought of saying goodbye to my brother should have alerted me to the counterfeit nature of my religiosity at the time, but I was too in love with my illusions to notice. I had become intoxicated with the unheard melodies of the monastery, those songs celebrating the mighty deeds I would carry out in God's service. I was so enchanted by these sirens that I could not see they only spelt shipwreck. My brother was just beginning to tackle his bowl of cornflakes when I walked up to the breakfast table and solemnly announced: "I'm going away to be a monk — for good." All he could summon up at that hour of the morning was a bemused, "well, if that's what you're into . . .," followed by an unconvincing "good luck." I had packed all my worldly possessions into a large brown soft-leather briefcase. Inside were squashed undergarments, pajamas, one shirt, one pair of trousers, two pairs of socks, a pair of brown sandals, a paperback edition of the New Testament, a new toothbrush and a fresh tube of toothpaste. There was no shampoo — I proposed to use monastery issue soap. Neither was there a shaving kit — I had not even begun to grow facial hair.

Although I was courageously giving my life away, I insisted on leaving the house through the back door for fear of the prying eyes of neighbors. I climbed silently into the back of the car, while my father and mother took the front seats. We headed north along the coast road, passing sleepy villages and towns, heading toward Mellifont Abbey near the Boyne Valley. As we neared our destination, my mother began to sob more frequently. My father hardly spoke a word.

The car turned into the entrance avenue. The wheels crunched on the gravel underneath as we cruised up to the monastery. Was my father deliberately driving at funereal pace? When a forbidding building came into view, perched on a naked hill, my mother exclaimed, "you could at least have chosen a human place to come. Not this barren, exposed monstrosity." "Precisely," I thought. "If you leave the world, you must really quit it. No half-measures. No cozy, cushy numbers. No cheap grace."

We were ushered into the guest room and sat uneasily awaiting the abbot. My mother had almost run out of Kleenex. My father's voice tried to soothe and reassure. I did a double take when the head monk arrived. It was not the same man who had been in charge six weeks before. The previous abbot had been a gentle, avuncular figure who yielded to my fervent desire to become a monk, despite his misgivings about my young age. A new boss meant new rules, a different ball game.

A decisive-looking man, he cast a quick glance at me, my puzzled father and most of all my distraught mother. She wiped her eyes: "Father Abbot, he is coming here for life. He's too young. He should never do this. But he won't listen. It's too late."

"It's certainly not too late, Mrs. Casey. In fact, it is too early. We couldn't possibly take him at the age of 17."

"Oh, thank God, thank God. I knew it. I told you all along, Tom." Her tears became sobs of joy.

My jaw dropped a few inches. I was truly crestfallen. The script had changed completely. How many times had I read of the saints of old entering the cloister, saying good-bye in the face of the vain entreaties and futile lamentations of their mothers?

"You could certainly stay a month here, see what it's like, live the life of a monk, but as for joining, you'd have to wait a few years," declared Father Abbot.

"That's just what he needs," my mother interjected. She turned to me in a loud whisper, "that will soon cure you of your infatuation with monasticism."

I stayed barely three weeks in the monastery. It took me even less time to realize how unsuited I was for this life. I did not find the adventure I had hoped for in monastic existence. Everything about the place was cruelly real. The buildings were bare, the food simple, the liturgies unadorned. Each morning I rose a few minutes before the birds and spent the day shoveling manure, building makeshift fences, and vacuuming the corridors. In this tiny world, I became sensitized to things that had not cost me a thought previously. I found it jarring to hear someone singing out of tune in choir, slurping over their soup or burping after dinner. But apart from the little details, I found the whole picture a turn-off. Life in the monastery was dull. Sure, the monks were good men, salt of the earth. But I wanted to be a light of the world. I wanted to see its sparkle. The cloister was too small for the epic life I envisaged. I certainly could take normalcy in reasonable doses. For instance I did not mind eating potatoes, even daily. But God save me from a mindless life of painfully peeling them for love of God and my brethren over a rusty kitchen sink.

It was because I had fallen in love with God that I went to the monastery in the first place. I had grown up in a Catholic household, which gave me a solid foundation in faith. As an adolescent I met other Catholic teenagers who enthused about God, read the Bible, enjoyed going to mass and praying together. That is when my own faith took off. I felt a new self because of this buoyant "we" gathered around me. And God's love for me began to feel alive and real. I prayed for an hour each day in my final year at school and happily attended daily mass.

But conversion was nevertheless a process. It did not happen instantly. God's way of leading me was to bring me on a journey. My human nature was not sufficiently developed for grace to build promisingly upon it. Perhaps for some people grace leap-frogs over nature, but in my case God's temple was not going to be built so quickly. It had to be constructed in a more painstaking and gradual way. I still had not had enough experience of life to construct a solid human foundation to support God's working in my heart.

And the danger was that without this solid basis, the whole edifice of grace might collapse. I still had not come to terms with my mixed reasons for wanting to become a monk, the fears that drove me as well as the idealism that fired me. As Saint Thomas Aquinas put it: "young people and drunks are indeed unsteady in reality, but in their own estimation they are more than capable, since they are not aware of their shortcomings." (*Summa Theologica* Ia IIae 40, 6)

I had gone to Mount Mellifont to immerse myself in peace, to get well away from the hassles of the world. I expected this Trappist monastery to catapult my inner life into orbit. Most of all I assumed it would deliver me from myself. But I was the same Tom inside the monastery as outside. Although I was in a peaceful place, it was still the same worried me inside. I had not suddenly become the picture of serenity. I had secretly hoped that the complexity of the world and my own struggling humanity might not have crossed the threshold of the cloister. But there was no enchanting transformation from ugly duckling into beautiful swan. Not even the feeling of being a more contented duckling.

The monastery was surrounded by rolling hills and patchwork green fields. But I was so topsy-turvy inside that I rarely stopped to watch the grazing cows dipping their heads into clumps of grass. Once or twice I glimpsed the hazy sun peeping between two sides of a narrow bar of cloud. I hardly ever listened to the upbeat song of blackbirds perched on the birch saplings. The June earth was heaving and popping all around me, and I felt like I had just imprisoned myself for a long winter. I trudged mindlessly over soft carpets of freshly-cut grass, dimly aware of the heavy sweet aroma. A fiery red fox poked its curious head out between the gaps of a low hedge to look at me as I walked worriedly under an overhanging elm tree. A brown spider was artfully ornamenting a wooden gate with dew-laden cobwebs that creased in the breeze, but I rushed past like the wind on fire. Older and wiser monks took time to contemplate. They walked peacefully along the evening avenue, admiring the dazzling patterns of starlings criss-crossing the soft orange sky, in slender lines and unlikely angles that were silhouetted against the deep red hue of the setting sun.

Although I only half found God in the monastery, God found me. He rewarded my flawed and foolish act of generosity with a much greater gift: himself. Although the demise of my promising monastic vocation did throw me off balance momentarily, I bounced back with the resilience of youth and tried again. Or more precisely, the Spirit of God tried to touch me once again and succeeded despite my blindness, and so I found myself entering the Society of Jesus.

Of course everything could have turned out differently. I suspect the devil tempted me to dream I could succeed in this way of life with the ulterior motive of seeing my attempt not only end in failure but also in a sense of discouragement about ever trying a vocation again. The devil is no fool, and he chooses the form of temptation that has the highest possibility of success. Therefore, if we are generous, he sometimes incites us to be excessively generous by spurring us to undertake actions that exceed our capabilities. The book of Proverbs wisely observes: "There is a way that seems right to a man, but in the end it leads to death" (Proverbs 16:25).

I took to the Jesuit spirit from the beginning: it allowed me to pray and meet God without having to withdraw myself physically from the world. Ignatius of Loyola (1491-1556) stressed that the world was not a loveless, graceless place; instead it was a place where God was at work. He gave extraordinary importance to even the smallest experiences, because he knew that God was speaking to him through the little details of everyday life. Ignatius paid especial attention to the desires and longings of the human heart. Desires are affective movements that draw us out of ourselves, and connect us to things and people around us. There is a strain in spirituality that regards desires with suspicion and hostility, as perilous obstacles to spiritual progress: it follows that a central task of the spiritual life is to curb and bridle them. Ignatius saw things differently. He realized that our desires were too miserly and superficial; they needed to be liberated from their constricted orbit. He knew that most people dared too little in their lives: they had become complacent and conformist, aspiring to the sixteenth-century equivalent of a lucrative career, trophy wife and detached house in the suburbs. True desire urges us ever onwards, refusing to rest in the comforts of domesticity or profit; it is nomadic, a pilgrim longing for what "no eye has seen, no mind has conceived" (1 Corinthians 2:9).

Without desires we would be less than human, we would lack the energy to move out of ourselves, and would find nothing to attract or motivate us. Ignatius did not reject the world of desires, he did not try to separate desires from religion and religious love. Instead he took desires so seriously that he sought to order and orient them in the most fulfilling direction possible: toward the greater glory of God. He clearly understood the need to channel desires in

the direction of goodness. He saw that holy desires consti-
tuted an imaginative way in which God cajoled individuals
beyond egoism and into love. Ignatius wanted to build on
the noblest and most generous desires, the desires to do
great things for God and for others.

Not all desires reach an epic scale; many are not of
earth-shattering consequence. In the course of a single day
we experience innumerable desires, many of which are not
life-changing: the desire to get up, work, eat, exercise, sleep
and so on. But the deepest desires within form the language
of the soul, a language which expresses an infinite longing:
we always want more than human life can offer us, we constantly desire something greater than all the money and success in the world, we incessantly yearn for a happiness that
will be without limits. And it is through nourishing these
huge desires that we expand our own capacity to embrace
and receive happiness. To become pure means refusing to
let our desires be limited by the petty idols around us,
because sooner or later they vanish: empires pass away,
celebrities become nobodies, and money turns into dust. All
these would-be divinities cannot escape decline and death.
But the desire for God defies death because it is attuned to
the voice of immortality: "if anyone keeps my word, he will
never see death" (John 8:51).

It was a number of years before I returned to the Boyne
Valley where life is less frenetic, where you speed past a
rickety milk lorry that clatters and chimes with crates and
bottles, as winding hedge-lined roads uncurl the way toward
Newgrange, an ancient megalithic passage tomb that has
become a major Irish tourist attraction. I was too embarrassed to drop into Mellifont itself but at least I was nearby,

in this same fertile part of the countryside that has been a focal point of religious interest from time immemorial.

I remember walking up the bright green meadow that led joyously to Newgrange, this fascinating monument which is over 5,000 years old, built shortly before the Egyptian pyramids. My eyes were caught by the spiraling lines and lozenges on the massive stone guarding its entrance. The spinning circles are as enigmatic as the crooked smile that plays upon Mona Lisa's lips. Nobody really knows what they stand for. Perhaps they are characters from the alphabet of a long forgotten language. Given the fact that this monument pre-dates the pyramids, one impish tourist suggested that it was graffiti written by construction workers of the time: "Job done, gone to Egypt!"

A narrow passage, about 60 feet long, leads inside to a cruciform chamber where people of ancient times placed the remains of the dead. Newgrange is a burial site for the dead that speaks of life. Over the entrance is a square hole which lets the sunlight in at dawn on the five shortest days of the year. If there are no clouds obstructing the sun on those mornings it sends a narrow beam into the passage that races along its length and illuminates the central chamber inside. On the shortest and darkest day of the year, December 21, the dawn brings new hope. Darkness and death give way to light and life.

The Book of Genesis tells us that in the beginning the earth was a wasteland devoid of form and that the primordial ocean was covered in darkness. Over the waters a mighty wind or spirit moved and blew. At the beginning no definitive direction had yet been taken and for that reason everything was still possible. What kind of pattern would the Spirit weave together from these waters of chaos?

Jeronimo Nadal, one of the first Jesuits and best interpreters of Ignatius of Loyola, once said that God guided Ignatius gently in a direction which he did not know. That strikes a chord in my own experience. Although I can make out the immediate steps ahead, I am never sure where the road is finally taking me. Many times I would have loved to be clearer about what I am destined to do. But more and more I can see that this desire for knowledge of the future is really a hidden yearning to control the things to come. I am invited to leave the future in the more than capable hands of God.

During my brief and doomed infatuation with monasticism, I forced myself to believe that being a monk was *the* way for me. By the time I stood at Newgrange, I knew that things had become clearer in the intervening few years. I had not found a magic faith chiseled with large letters in the stone of the monastery. Even though the prospect of life in a remote hermitage had once seemed heavenly, now I felt more attracted to the sound of the city, the roar of Harley Davidsons, and the rush of people on crowded streets. I was intrigued with meeting people like the drenched drug addict outside a derelict pub who abruptly tells you about his image of God. "If there is a God then it is someone like me ma, coming around when I'm going through cold turkey, and asking me 'how are ya?'" Although I could not quite get monasticism or mysticism out of my system, I preferred the tinny sound of a crumpled Coke can to the hushed silence of green grass or glum gravel underfoot.

After the Spirit of God hovers over the waters at the beginning of Genesis, God says, "let there be light." I had sought out the monastery to help me find God. I had withdrawn from what I regarded as a godless world and fled to a God I thought was worldless. Reality was much more complex and exciting. I needed to get in touch with the fragmented lives of people and my own fragmentation. That is where I would find God — in less obvious places.

You stand talking to a drug addict who looks like a drowned rat and the rain pours down upon you as well, streaming through your hair, running down the slope of your nose. The moment of sacramental baptism is crucial. It is the sacred beginning of an incredible journey. But there is also a time when what it means to be a man for others hits home. A moment when you realize whom God is calling you to serve in the here and now. Standing there in the damp chill of an Irish day, your hair soaked with rain and your woolen pullover heavy with the wet, you might be graced by an epiphany.

I still had a tiny image of God when I left the monastery. I had not accepted that my image of myself was too big and idealistic. Part of purification is the constant enlargement of my image of God, an image that will never do justice to the infinity of his life and love. To become purified, I need God's grace. It is tempting to retain the implicit and unspoken assumption that I can bring my own conversion to its term. In fact I cannot, and if I delude myself that I can, I fall prey to narcissism. The exercise of personal willpower will not bring me salvation. Because I once fed excessively on a diet of James Bond films and big-action blockbusters, I have to remind myself frequently and insistently that I do not produce my own redemption.

The model of the heroic outsider is strong in the popular mythology of Western culture, a figure with special and exceptional powers who uses violence to redeem the community from evil and circumvents dubious laws and failed institutions. Because of the pervasive presence of this hero-ic paradigm in film and literature, it is almost natural to think that strong-arm tactics will also bring success in the spiritual sphere. But in the life of the spirit we cannot rid the world of evil with Uzi submachine guns. In fact, to make any progress at all in the life of the spirit, we have to bite the bullet and confess that we are not cool clean super-heroes or even paragons of virtue, but on the contrary, part of the problem. We too need to be cleansed.

To purify myself is to engage in a long and grace-assist-ed task of stripping myself of much of the dross that I uncritically take to be essential. The love that animates purification is not sentimental; rather it is the capacity to reach out beyond myself and seek the good of others. If my own agenda and my own needs predominate at the expense of the interests of Christ, I know I am still at the beginning.

Purity is something we never fully achieve. We can never sit back in smug self-satisfaction. We need to stay alert and vigilant for purity is always something beyond us, something we have not arrived at, and something we will never definitively realize. We always struggle to remain faithful, and temptations never go away. But at the same time through our good will, which is expressed in our lov-ing fidelity to God's commandments, we advance toward our destination. God is continually turned in our direction with a look full of love which invites us into communion with him, for free: this is what grace is. And grace is some-thing we could never have come up with ourselves. As Hamlet says to the more pedestrian Horatio, there are things out there which are not dreamt of in any philosophy. Grace is something undeserved and could never be earned, even with the most ardent efforts. It is always the free gift of love, which enables us to love in our turn. And the more we love, the more God reveals himself to us, until one day we scale the heights and dive into his endless depth.

Great music is graceful: it adds something unexpected to what is fundamentally a limited collection of notes, and what it gives us is something we never earned, something in a sense we have no right or claim to. A piano conjures up images of astonishing beauty with a handful of notes, a violin whispers mystifying dreams, a cello soothes and reassures. There are certain melodies and songs that touch me in ways I could never have predicted or imagined; there are tunes that have helped me see my life in a deeper and richer way; there are songs that pop up unannounced from my memory banks having been dormant there since childhood. And these rhythms and melodies do not move me because of anything I have done: it is not as if I suddenly said, "I want this particular song to affect me deeply now." No, it simply happens that way, without any bidding on my part. That is grace: a gift I never dreamed of that does not come about through my own efforts but arrives from someone larger and more loving than myself. It is a gift that humbles me: I get a sense of how much mystery there is in life and how little of this mystery I have recognized, a sense of the great generosity of God in the light of which my own response seems miserly by comparison.

Angels are also associated with music and singing. At the birth of Jesus, the angels could not contain their joy. They proclaimed God's glory, announcing peace to people of good will. I like to imagine that they sang this message or at least proclaimed it in melodious voices more harmonious and musical than any choir or instrument could be. Not being an angel myself, I have at times felt hesitant about the beauty of music. On entering the Jesuits as a young and impressionable teenager, I decided it would be best to leave my guitar at home. I felt that playing music would be too self-indulgent and worldly a pursuit in religious life. When I happened to mention this resolution to the master of novices, he ordered me *not* to arrive at the novitiate without my guitar. I am glad he treasured this invisible and intangible sound we call music. The Jesuit priest and poet Gerard Manley Hopkins (1844-1889) burned his early poems after entering the Jesuits, because he could not reconcile them with his religious calling. Luckily he had a change of heart later, and left us poems with such innovative rhythms that they cry out to be sung. Hopkins claimed his poetic voice and sang his song. Each of us has a unique song to sing, our own song, the one designed for our voice, bearing the imprint of our character, revealing the path of our destiny. It is a song God has already hummed for us from eternity.

People do not always sing their song: they confuse love with sex and religion with addiction, and end up looking for pleasure or a fix rather than the pearl of hidden price. We need to dig beneath superficial versions of purity in order to find the hidden treasure. This is what we turn to in the next chapter.

2

Bleakness to Bounty

In the sixth month, God sent the angel Gabriel to Nazareth, a town in Galilee, to a virgin pledged to be married to a man named Joseph, a descendant of David. The virgin's name was Mary.

Luke 1: 26-27

My bounty is as boundless as the sea,
My love as deep; the more I give to thee,
The more I have, for both are infinite.

Juliet in William Shakespeare's
Romeo and Juliet Act 2, Scene II

Although we often imagine angels singing or playing musical instruments, I like to think that there are times when they are silent. One of those moments was the silent pause of the angel Gabriel after inviting the Virgin Mary to be the mother of Jesus. Not only was Gabriel silent; the whole heavenly choir interrupted their singing while the prophets and patriarchs strained to hear with bated breath. Even the three divine Persons, full of respect for the freedom of this young Jewish girl, watched to see what Mary's response would be. And when Mary gave her "yes", her "fiat," there was an explosion of joy in the whole universe. All the angels praised God for the wonder of his love and mercy in sending his only Son into the world as Savior and Messiah. Humankind was moving from bleakness to bounty.

It is ironic that purity is more often associated with bleakness than with bounty, especially because the extraordinary richness and disarming generosity of Christ's coming among us occurred in and through the purity of the Virgin Mary, "the noblest gem in Christianity after Christ" (Martin Luther, Christmas sermon, 1531). Purity is inseparably linked with life and fullness. The biggest lie about purity is that it is soul-destroying and life-denying.

Although purity has a bad name when it comes to religion, in other realms of life that do not touch us so deeply, it is valued. We approve of purity in matters of food, drink, personal hygiene, appearance, the arts, and so on. Let's take some examples: the internal hygiene of fasting is about *purifying* the body by ridding it of wastes and toxins, in order to improve health and even prolong the life-span. When it comes to what we actually eat, we witness a steady rise in the popularity of organic food in the Western world because consumers believe it is *purer* than conventional produce and free from fertilizers, artificial pesticides, and growth hormones. As for drinking habits, there has been a huge shift to bottled water in recent years, primarily because consumers perceive it as *pure*, a perception reinforced by labels that depict crystal-clear alpine springs and virginal glaciers. Alcohol too is valued for its purity: German breweries still adhere to the medieval *"purity law"* or *Reinheitsgebot*, which insists that only pure and indispensable ingredients — malt, hops, yeast and water —

should be used to make beer. Purity also plays an important role in external hygiene. Since time immemorial *hand-washing* has been associated with purity. In our own day outbreaks of bugs and viruses in hospitals are regularly linked with the failure of medical staff to wash their hands. Not only hands must be seen to be clean; the entire body is more attractive when it has a pure appearance. Beauty is more than skin-deep, but *clear skin* is valued for its purity from blemishes and stains. In the world of cosmetics, companies never advertise impure beauty products, because they know that women want a beauty that is pure. Italian culture lays great stress on *la bella figura*, so much so that cutting a beautiful figure before the eyes of the world is a cultural imperative there. In the arts purity is revered: people queue up and pay high prices on Broadway in order to have a *pure* theatre experience; diehard classical music fans want it *pure* and are unhappy at the idea of fusing classical with jazz and other genres. In sports, football coaches often insist on holding crucial team practices behind closed doors, in order to keep out distractions and media hoopla and help teams focus *purely* and exclusively on an upcoming match. In the realm of intellectual endeavor, *pure mathematics*, which is carried out without immediate concerns about its direct application, still thrives at universities worldwide. When it comes to the animal world, people go to extraordinary expense and energy to breed the best *thoroughbred* horses from the finest bloodlines available.

These examples show that we still attach value to purity in many realms of life; it is not simply an outdated practice from the religions and rites of primitive cultures. And we use the term in many different spheres, yet there is an overlapping of meanings — purity evokes something that is unmixed, without stain, single-minded, focused, and transparent. Even though the examples I chose are more random than representative, it is telling that in each case purity is regarded as something positive — good, valuable, praiseworthy and desirable. What is even more striking is the fact that when we turn to the religious sphere, purity evokes predominantly negative impressions — austerity, denial, inhibition, prudery, and priggishness. Religious purity is seen as something moralistic and repressive, an unfair and unjustified restriction of love. Literary and cinematic portrayals often serve to reinforce this impression.

The famous French short story writer Guy de Maupassant (1850-1893) once wrote a touching fable, "Clair de Lune," about a priest called Father Marignan, a tall, thin, self-righteous cleric, whose zeal knew no bounds. He was convinced he knew the mind of God, and occasionally as he paced up and down his garden he would ask himself why God had done a particular thing. He would dwell on the question relentlessly, putting himself in God's shoes, as it were, and nine times out of ten would come up with an answer. Father Marignan inhabited an ordered and predictable world, believing that day and night as well as summer and winter alternated according to the needs of humanity and agriculture.

This priest also despised women. He looked on woman as the temptress who had led man astray in the beginning and as far as he was concerned she had done so ever since, not just because of her body which drew man to perdition but even more because of her loving soul and her confounded tenderness. In fact he believed that God had created woman expressly in order to tempt and try man. He only approached women with the greatest of caution. He was severe and aloof even with nuns, yet the tenderness of their voices and gestures touched him despite his best efforts to shield himself.

Father Marignan had a niece who lived nearby with her mother. He was intent on making the girl a nun. Sometimes he went for walks with her and told her about his God, but his niece never listened. She gazed up at the sky, looked at the flowers and the grass, her eyes full of joy and life. Whenever he got annoyed with her she gave him a hug, and while part of him wanted to pull free of her embrace, another part enjoyed the fatherly feeling her affection drew forth.

One day the wife of the sacristan told him that his niece was in love. Father Marignan was so shocked that he initially refused to believe the news. The sacristan's wife assured him that what she said was true, and added that the young couple met each evening before midnight down by the river.

All day long Father Marignan fumed inside. That night he picked up his large cane and prepared to leave his house with the intention of confronting the couple and putting an end to the affair. He opened the front door, but hesitated on the threshold, taken aback by the beauty of the moonlight, which had never shone with such splendor before. And because there was something of the poet and dreamer inside of him, he felt suddenly distracted, moved by the tranquil beauty of the pallid night. He walked through the garden, inhaling long and deeply, imbibing the air, full of wonder and delight, practically forgetting all about his niece in the process.

Once outside the garden, he found himself halting to contemplate the moonlight that streamed across the plain. He could hear the regular metallic sound of a cricket and further away the nightingales dispersed their quivering music into the night, a music that sounded as though it were created for love. The priest continued to make his way, but now his heart failed within him and he was overcome by a sense of exhaustion. He simply wanted to stop and be still and behold the beauty of God in his creation.

As was his custom, Father Marignan put himself a question about God. Since the night was made for slumber and oblivion, since nobody was awake to see it, he asked himself why God had made it more enchanting than the day and why it revealed things too mysterious and fine for the bright light of the sun. He could find no answer.

As he continued to puzzle over this, he caught sight of two figures walking side by side under the trees. The man had his arm around the woman and now and then kissed her on the forehead. The couple radiated life to the natural world that surrounded them, and they appeared to the priest as a single entity for whom the beauty of this serene night was intended. They walked in his direction as though God had sent them as the living response to his question.

The priest stopped, his heart beating strongly, and found words of love from the Song of Songs ringing in his ears. And he thought to himself that perhaps God provided nights such as these to give a perfect setting and frame for human love. He pulled back from the still advancing couple, even though it was his own niece in the arms of this man. He felt he might be disobeying God were he to interfere. He began to suspect that it was God who allowed and encouraged love since he gave the beauty of this luminous night to envelop it. After a moment Father Marignan turned and walked away, shamefaced and embarrassed, feeling he had invaded a temple which he had no right to enter.

Purity has nothing to do with the misogynistic, fearful, legalistic, and self-righteous attitude we find in Father Marignan at the beginning of de Maupassant's short story. Christians believe in love and beauty. And any man with reason should thank God for the gift of women. Yet the evidence of literature, cinema and life would seem to suggest that distortions of purity, not to mention self-deception concerning it, are occupational hazards for Christian priests and ministers. The French writer André Gide (1869-1951) shows the tragic and evil consequences of self-delusion about purity in his short novel *La Symphonie Pastorale*. Despite the unevenness of the novel, Gide does at least succeed in masterfully describing how a naïve Swiss pastor's initial impulse of Christian charity toward a blind orphan girl gradually and almost imperceptibly metamorphoses into lust.

Ingmar Bergman's 1982 masterpiece *Fanny and Alexander*, which marked his farewell to cinema direction, shows an unappealing aberration of purity in the figure of a Swedish Lutheran bishop. The film is set in the opening decade of the twentieth century, and tells the story of the prosperous Ekdahl family, whose members run a provincial theatre. After her husband Oscar dies of a stroke, his beautiful widow Emilie, the leading actress in the theatre he directed, turns to Bishop Edvard Vergérus for comfort, and quickly falls in love with him. To the dismay of her two young children, the 10 year old Alexander and his slightly younger sister Fanny, Emilie accepts the bishop's proposal of marriage. Emilie also agrees to give up her career as an actress. Before the wedding ceremony, the bishop also stipulates that she and her children must bring absolutely nothing with them when they move into his episcopal palace —

no clothes, furniture, books, jewelry or toys. He demands that Emilie even relinquish her former friends, habits and thoughts. He wants them to leave their previous life completely behind, in order to live purely before the face of God.

The contrast between the sumptuous life of the Ekdahl household and the deathly austerity of the bishop's palace could not be more pronounced. Bishop Edvard tells Emilie that out of respect for his predecessors, he has kept the house in an unaltered state, and adds that they should all be grateful for the privilege of living in an ambience marked by purity and severity. The bishop's unmarried sister, one of several intimidating inhabitants in this puritanical household, explains to Emilie and the children during their first unappetizing meal that punctuality, cleanliness and order are the reigning values there.

This severe prelate thinks of himself as the quintessence of enlightenment and liberality. Because love makes her blind, Emilie also initially idealizes the handsome cleric. She interprets his authoritarianism as benevolence and fails to see the cruel streak in his character. A hard-fought battle of wills develops between the young Alexander and his new stepfather. The boy hates the bishop and this hatred contributes to bringing the worst aspects of the prelate's character into play. Although it is hard at times not to feel sympathy for the tortured personality of the bishop, the viewer almost heaves a sigh of relief when retribution strikes him. Despite the good intentions that Edvard undoubtedly possesses, the film unmasks his savage brutality.

Given these clerical exaggerations and distortions that we find not only in the literary and cinematic world, but also in real life, a legalistic and moralizing vocabulary is too restrictive when it comes to purity. This vocabulary is weighed down by too many "oughts" and "shoulds", and its horizon is too narrow. Purity needs space to breathe in all its energizing life. It needs a large and liberating context in which to thrive. It is time to go beyond tired platitudes about purity. If we can enter that larger space, then the deeper meaning of purity can be found, one that makes us free because it is the story of the hunger to love and be loved.

For centuries there has been an unhappy strain in ethical and religious thought that has banned pleasure and joy from morality. It is already present in the Stoic thinkers of Greek and Roman antiquity, who recommended resignation to fate and the purging of passions and emotions. It is spelled out and codified by Immanuel Kant (1724-1804) who believed that moral acts lose their value if people perform them in order to get joy. Although God loves cheerful givers (2 Corinthians 9:7), Kant had no time for them. The Prussian philosopher was suspicious of happiness and delight; at most he allowed them as unintended consequences of our actions. He preached duty and disinterest instead. But the truth is that human beings need happiness and pleasure. To empty morality of pleasure is to go against nature. The human being who cannot enjoy doing good things is simply not good.

Unfortunately, the practice of Christianity has often been contaminated by a legalistic and duty-bound morality. Christians can too easily forget that Jesus summed up and encapsulated the Good News in the commandment to love. Although love is a commandment, it is not one that is externally imposed. It is animated from the inside, it surges from the heart, and it enriches us with joy. Ideally Christians do

49

not have joy as their ultimate goal; nevertheless they receive it as the natural companion of love. If we love we will experience joy and delight. And the fact that loving brings such joy is an added incentive to seek the good of God and others. Indeed, the more joy we experience in loving, the more we will want to love.

In this chapter I have been trying to render the music of purity by contrast, by showing what it is not, through describing songs that falsify it. Now it is time to change key and look at prayer, as I describe how I begin each day, asking God to help me in the quest to become pure.

3

Healed through an Angel

*Then one of the seraphs flew to me with a live coal
in his hand, which he had taken with tongs from the
altar.*

(Isaiah 6:6)

*From the ashes a fire shall be woken,
A light from the shadows shall spring;
Renewed shall be blade that was broken:
The crownless again shall be king.*

J.R.R. Tolkien, *The Lord of the Rings*

The Gospel of Matthew tells us that Joseph decided to separate from Mary privately when he found out she was pregnant. This just man was dismayed when he mistakenly
thought that Mary had betrayed him. Being the good man he
was, he probably initially refused to believe that Mary could
be expecting; yet as the days wore by, the evidence became
undeniable. He could visualize his good name being
destroyed and see himself becoming the butt of the snide
remarks of his neighbors. And meanwhile his love for Mary
grew cold, his respect for her crumbled, as he faced the

incontrovertible evidence of his senses — the woman to whom he had pledged himself was already with child. Had Joseph not been a man of such extraordinary integrity, he would no doubt have publicly denounced Mary as an adulteress. Had he taken this step, Mary might have been stoned, and the unborn Jesus would have died with her. Instead Joseph went through anguish and pain, and having prayed to God, decided to separate quietly from Mary. He went to sleep and while he was sleeping,

> an angel of the Lord appeared to him in a dream and said, "Joseph son of David, do not be afraid to take Mary home as your wife, because what is conceived in her is from the Holy Spirit. She will give birth to a son, and you are to give him the name Jesus, because he will save his people from their sins" (Matthew 1:20-21).

Joseph's doubts were healed by the words of the angels, his fears dispelled. He felt a mixture of joy, awe, and pain. He was overjoyed that the Son of God was to be born in his humble household. He was full of awe at the prospect. He was also deeply pained that he had doubted Mary and that he had been on the point of abandoning her. Joseph aged humanly during that short time of trial, but he also grew greatly in the purity of his love.

In a less dramatic way, I am continually healed by the words of an angel: each day I am humbled by the message of a heavenly being. My story is tied up with a vision of the prophet Isaiah, a vision I contemplate before my mind's eye each morning in prayer. But before describing this heavenly vision, I want to say something about the timing of my daily prayer, which is of great significance in the context of purity, because if I am to give God the best of myself, I also have to give him the best of myself in prayer.

It was through the story of Cain and Abel that I learned how to give God my "first fruits" in prayer. Jealousy, wounded pride, anger, and above all murder are words that come to mind when we hear the names of the two brothers Cain and Abel. The tragic story of the first fratricide in history unfolds in Chapter 4 of Genesis. The elder son of Adam and Eve, filled with rage that the offering of his younger brother Abel is accepted while God gives no importance to his own, vents his fury on Abel in a cold and premeditated manner, arranging to meet him in a field, and while there Cain rises up against Abel and kills him. Cain is punished by God and condemned to lead the life of a fugitive, wandering the earth without ever finding a place called home (although in a profound act of compassion, God sets a mark upon Cain so that he may be protected from the violence of others). There is no explicit reason given for why God prefers Abel's offering to that of Cain. It does not seem to be linked to their different occupations: after all, both had respectable callings, farming the earth and herding sheep. Indeed their occupations were already anticipated in the heavenly Garden of Eden that their parents at first inhabited: like his father Adam who cultivated the earth, Cain was a tiller of the soil, while Abel's vocation as a shepherd was in line with Adam being entrusted dominion over the animal kingdom. My hunch is that God's sympathy with Abel's offering and his dissatisfaction with what Cain brought were connected with the different kinds of gifts they presented to God, and the attitudes that these diverse tributes revealed. It is in this half-hidden aspect of the Cain and Abel story that I find a daily source of inspiration.

Abel brought God the firstlings of his flock of sheep, while Cain just presented the Lord with any old fruit from the ground, but not the first and not the finest. Perhaps Cain only gave God what was left over when he had satisfied his own needs; maybe he even presented it grudgingly or calculatingly, merely in order to appease God or to keep on good terms or as a way of ensuring he would receive something in return. Abel's motivation, however, was not self-interested. Had Abel's focus been solely on his flock, he would no doubt have been tempted to give an old sheep to God, one that would have been of little practical use to him. But instead Abel made a personal sacrifice by giving his first and best. Abel's primary focus was on God. He was grateful to God for the blessings of his flock and he expressed his gratitude sincerely and from the depths of his heart. Abel's generous act inspires me.

Each morning I try to follow Abel's example in a small and practical way. When I awaken, I sit up in my bed, and give the "first fruits" of the day to God, by giving my heart and my attention to him before I give my energy or time to anything or anybody else. I know from Abel's oblation that this offering is pleasing to God. Although this practice helps me and I am happy to share this story with you, I am not implying that you should go out and do the same. But on the other hand, it is worth considering . . . I guess there are many people who find that their best time to give God is later in the day, in the tranquil hours of the evening, when the world is hushed and work has drawn to a close. In my case, the first hour is best.

I used to be like Cain in the sense that formerly I gave God the time that was left over when all my other priorities had been taken care of. Prayer often came at the end of a busy day when I was exhausted or else it was squeezed between "urgent" tasks that regularly claimed my attention during the time of prayer itself. Either way I had little energy to focus on God. In cultivating the land, Cain perhaps made his own plot, built fences around it, and began to see the plants that grew there as his own creation. Maybe he made his plot into a little "god", something that claimed all his care and attention. In focusing on my schedule, I saw each day and its activities as dependent on me, as issuing from me. I made my little plan into a god of sorts, and unfortunately relegated the one true God to an afterthought. Like Cain, I began to realize that my offering was not pleasing to God. In the biblical story, God speaks to Cain, reasoning with him and trying to encourage him. This direct communication with Cain is a testimony to God's love for him — interestingly, there is no record of God speaking to his younger brother Abel. God does not tell Cain that he rejects his offering. He simply tells him that his offering has been put on hold, as it were, until Cain sorts out his priorities and starts doing what is right. For my part, I felt God speaking to my heart and saying: "I am glad that you give time to prayer, but why not be really generous and offer me the first fruits of your day?"

If I start off my day with Jesus, I find I am more likely to continue the day in his presence. As an old Irish saying puts it, "a good start is half the battle." In the morning I consecrate to the Lord my day and all that will unfold during it. If I postpone my hour of prayer until later, it can easily fall by the wayside because of numerous and often unscheduled claims on my time. Certainly in the evening I take time out to give thanks to God, but there is something special about the first hour of the day: it evokes new birth and renewal. A beloved saying of salespeople goes, "you don't get a second chance to make a first impression." And I know that I want to make the first impression of the day on God, by offering him the first fruits. The second best is never good enough for God. He deserves so much more. And if what I give God does not mean much to me, how can I realistically expect that it will mean anything to him?

To begin, I recite some words from the prophet Isaiah that I have come to know by heart. They come from a passage that means a lot to me. It tells the story of a grand vision of Isaiah, yet despite the grandeur of this vision, its message keeps me humble and real. It is a vivid reminder of my continual need for God and my constant need of purification. Here it is:

> In the year that King Uzziah died, I saw the Lord seated on a throne, high and exalted, and the train of his robe filled the temple. Above him were the seraphs, each with six wings: with two wings they covered their faces, with two they covered their feet, and with two they were flying. And they were calling to one another: "Holy, holy, holy is the LORD Almighty; the whole earth is full of his glory." At the sound of their voices the doorposts and thresholds shook and the temple was filled with smoke.

> "Woe is me!" I cried. "I am ruined! For I am a man of unclean lips, and I live among a people of unclean lips, and my eyes have seen the King, the LORD

Almighty." Then one of the seraphs flew to me with a live coal in his hand, which he had taken with tongs from the altar. With it he touched my mouth and said, "See, this has touched your lips; your guilt is taken away and your sin atoned for."

Then I heard the voice of the Lord saying, "Whom shall I send? And who will go for us?" And I said, "Here am I. Send me!" (Isaiah 6:1-8)

In the opening sentence, Isaiah notes that his momentous vision took place in the year that King Uzziah died. The death of this long-reigning king of Judah was truly the end of an era, and it caused apprehension and disquiet. Not just because the death of a king was a portentous event, since kings traditionally exercised a kind of power that echoed divine omnipotence; and not only because of uncertainty about what life under the new ruler would be like. The unease was also on account of the distressing final years of Uzziah, when he suffered a disease as a result of disobeying God. King Uzziah had become King of Judah as a teenager and ruled the kingdom for over half a century. For most of that time King Uzziah's track record was more than impressive: he fortified the defenses of Jerusalem, modernized the Judean army and extended the kingdom's territory. He brought stability and prosperity to the nation. But in his later years, swollen with pride, he flouted God's command by usurping the priestly role and burning incense on the altar of incense inside the Temple. His pride was his undoing. As a result he was struck down by disease and underwent the slow and humiliating death of a leper, banished from contact with his former subjects. The sad story is told in 2 Chronicles 26.

Isaiah had no doubt admired Uzziah as a youth, only to be taken aback by the king's pride and disobedience, and his sorry fate. And now he found himself in the same Temple where the deceased king had perpetrated his sacrilegious action. Perhaps Isaiah was praying for the dead king and for guidance as his nation entered a new and uncertain future. While he was there, Isaiah saw a new king, a different king, not an earthly and imperfect one, but a heavenly and perfect one. This king, seated upon a throne, has the attributes of divine majesty. It is the true King, Yahweh Sabaoth, who with a single smile created galaxy upon galaxy, who from his inexhaustible riches stretched jeweled stars across the heavens, and took human beings from the dust of the earth, enlivening them with the breath of life.

In Isaiah's vision, God was sitting upon a throne, the real king not only of Judah, but of the whole universe. Isaiah was obviously some distance from God, since he did not see him close up but high and exalted. God was beyond anything Isaiah could have conceived with his own mind: this was not a God that Isaiah could tame, domesticate, reduce or edit to his own petty dimensions. Beside God were angels of a special kind, "fiery ones" or "flaming ones," as the name seraphim suggests. The seraphim are the purest of all creatures, and so the ones who can stand closest to God. Although these heavenly beings were glorious in themselves, before the surpassing glory of God they had such reverence that they shielded their faces with two wings. Perhaps too these flaming beings had to protect themselves from the consuming fire of God, so holy as to burn them into nothingness by comparison. For in the face of God's holiness, every creature fades into insignificance. The great fire of these angels is utterly focused and dependent on the holy and ineffable fire of God, the fount of all energy and life in the universe. With another two wings the seraphim flew, an image of continual activity, complete availability, and ceaseless service.

And as Isaiah looked at this wondrous sight, he also heard the sound of these most noble of angels announcing God's holiness, and proclaiming the presence of his glory throughout the world. God's unalloyed and unconditional love distinguishes him from everything that is soiled and lacking in love; thus his holiness sets him radically apart from all living beings. This infinite qualitative difference between God and creation is one facet of the relationship between God and human beings. But it is also true that God's glory is manifested in the world and in the creatures of the world. The angels chanted that the glory of God was not simply confined to the Temple but shone forth through all of creation. The holiness of God is everywhere, and so sacredness and goodness can be found in every place; the extraordinary is also in the ordinary. God is simultaneously beyond the world, indescribably transcendent, and yet also in the world, in our midst, if only we have eyes to see. Beneath the dross of ordinary life, beneath its struggles and pains, there is an infinity of light shining forth, burning away evil with the glow of a goodness that will ultimately triumph, with the dazzling light that will destroy darkness. As Gerald Manley Hopkins would put it thousands of years later in his famous "God's Grandeur," a poem throbbing with life and light:

The world is charged with the grandeur of God
It will flame out, like shining from shook foil . . .

In New Testament times, the apostle John, in exile on
the small island of Patmos, because he would not stop proclaiming Jesus, instead of Caesar, as Lord, had a vision that
was similar to that of Isaiah. In Chapter 4 of Revelation,
John saw God in his glory upon a beautiful throne. John
also heard angelic beings continuously proclaiming God's
holiness. Night and day, they never tired of chanting "Holy,
Holy, Holy is the Lord God Almighty, who was, and is, and
is to come" (Revelation 4:8).

Hearing the sublime voices of the angels and witnessing the majesty of God, Isaiah simultaneously saw his own
inadequacy. Even the foundations of the immense edifice of
the Temple trembled and shook before the greatness of God.
The experience of God's power shows up our weakness.
The experience of true holiness is truly humbling. In fact,
Isaiah was so taken back at his own sinfulness that he
exclaimed, "I am ruined! For I am a man of unclean lips."
Isaiah's cry must have been like a painful echo of the cry
that escaped the lips of the former king Uzziah when he was
reduced to the status of a leper. Sin cannot survive the presence of God. Isaiah predicted his ruin, expecting punishment, suffering or death. But none of these fears were realized. God's holiness was greater than any sin of Isaiah's.
And furthermore, the God that Isaiah saw was not a vengeful or angry God, but a God full of compassion. He heard
the heartfelt and humble cry of Isaiah. Sitting there in all his
majesty, God was not deaf to the trembling voice of this
man who felt weighed down by his mortality and sin. God
was not cocooned in splendid and uncaring isolation. God

was infinitely more interested in Isaiah than the prophet had dared expect. God cared. And in a sublime demonstration of goodness and mercy, God immediately sent a seraphim to minister to this poor man. The angel arrived at Isaiah's side, holding a burning coal in his hand, which he had taken with tongs from the altar. Because angels are totally dedicated to God in obedient service, we know that this seraphim would never have dreamed of taking a flaming coal from the altar and bringing it to Isaiah of his own volition. The seraphim performed this merciful deed because God commanded him to do it. There was no price to pray for this healing gift. Purification was without charge. Isaiah was to be cleansed for free. The angel, being a perfect messenger, did not deliver his own message, but spoke the words of God: "See, this has touched your lips; your guilt is taken away and your sin atoned for." The purifying initiative issued from God, and the touch of burning coal and the fire of God's word healed Isaiah.

In an instant Isaiah's guilt was taken away and his sin forgiven. The purification at the hand of the angel gave Isaiah the possibility of access to God. There were no charred lips, there was no scorched tongue. The fiery coal from the heavenly altar did not physically burn Isaiah, since immediately afterwards he could speak without difficulty. And he did speak, responding to God's searching questions, "Whom shall I send? And who will go for us?" But what was different now was the way in which Isaiah talked and the things he said. Isaiah spoke in a new way, because the live coal had set his heart ablaze, and he was on fire with the desire to serve God by proclaiming his liberating good news. He was freed for service. He was willing to go on God's mission.

I recite these words from Isaiah each morning because I want to see things as they are. I want a vision of God's holiness that takes my breath away. Holiness is essentially love at its most pure, something which is unfathomably deep, like the glorified Jesus, "whose eyes are like blazing fire" (Revelation 2:18), and whose veiled majesty during his life on earth radiated holiness in a more bearable way. I want to see myself as I am, but without being discouraged by my littleness, for I place my hope in God. I hope this vision keeps me humble, though I know how easy it is to tell God I am nothing and how difficult it becomes to stomach this truth when a fellow human being confirms it to my face. So in order to become truly humble, I pray for humility with faith, confident that God can work this miracle for me. I want to adore, by acknowledging the greatness of God, source and summit of all goodness, while gladly affirming my dependence upon him. I want to be fascinated even though something within me trembles at the holiness of God, and threatens to become disheartened because of my own unworthiness. I do not want to run away in fear. I want to run forward in confidence. I want to be purified for service. I want to become holy myself, set myself aside for God's service, separate myself from sin, and become saturated with Christ and his love, "for it is written: 'be holy, because I am holy'" (1 Peter 1:16).

The vision of Isaiah also puts purity in its proper context for me. An angel flies to Isaiah's side and places a burning coal against his lips. There is nothing static or frigid about this picture: instead we have the dynamism and movement of the angel allied to the intense heat of a burning coal that touches Isaiah's lips. If some elements of this vision seem to have erotic undercurrents, I believe it is a sign that the pure person is called to be no less passionate about God than a lover is about his beloved. Indeed the passion and energy of this scenario transcend the vitality of erotic love. However deep the sexual drive may be, there are infinitely deeper forces at work inside of us: God himself is active inside us because each of us possesses a soul.

Because Isaiah seemingly has no sensation of soreness or burning afterwards, because he is able to speak, I take this picture to be that of a burning that is interior, invisible and spiritual rather than exterior, visible and material. But if someone were to try to capture this vision faithfully in a painting or on film, they could not but make it passionately alive. The scene of the angel touching Isaiah's lips is simply pulsing with life. This vision puts purity into an appropriate context because it shows that purity is not a life-denying negation of sex. Rather, purity is a life-affirming yes to the energy and passion that is found in sex, yet purity also brings this life to a higher, richer and more real level. Purity brings the life of sex to a more elevated expression for various reasons. For example, although purity is passionate, it is a passion devoid of egoism. Pure persons are not out to get something for themselves, there is nothing ego-driven about them. Purity is not cloying, self-centered, manipulative or calculating. But for all that there is nothing cold or lifeless about purity. It is ablaze: it is a burning fire. Sex is a faint ember compared to the intense heat and radiant light of purity. Sex is a momentary ray of light; purity is the sun itself, a ball of fire. Sex is a taste; purity is the whole restaurant with all the meals included. Sex is a snippet of song; purity is the greatest hits collection and the entire symphony rolled into one.

In fact purity is not necessarily linked to sex at all; purity has a much larger meaning. Unless we discern this vaster context, we will be unable to live purity in all its marvelous depth and enchanting transparency. For a Christian, purity means to be completely taken up by God, just as Isaiah was in saying "here I am," just as the apostle John was when he was literally taken up by the Spirit and saw the heavenly visions described in the Book of Revelation. Purity, then, is something that envelops our whole being.

It is in Jesus that we see purity at its most radiant. It is an intense flame that is constantly burning within him, spreading forth its flames to all around him. It is a spring that wells up from the depths of his heart and flows out as living water. What does Jesus' purity concretely mean? His boundless, consuming, unreserved love of the Father and of everyone and everything the Father loves. Jesus was not focused on himself, but on the Father. Nothing and nobody held him back from this self-surrendering love. Jesus gave everything. His nourishment was to do the will of the Father; upon this he fed. He did not yearn for wealth or power or sensual delights. He renounced anything and everything that would have been an obstacle to this love. At every moment of every day he was present to the Father.

Nobody else has been as pure as Jesus, true God and true man. In every second of his life, and with every fiber of his being Jesus stretched towards the Father, with a desire that had no limits. Jesus' purity was this undivided love, uncontaminated by any lesser interest or influence. One human being did attain utter purity as a creature — the Virgin Mary. Many of the mystical theologians of the first centuries after Christ were lavish in their praise of Mary's purity, calling her a tabernacle without defilement, the sealed fountain of the Holy Spirit, a lily springing among thorns, the New and Living Ark, the womb in which God pitched his tent among us. Closer to our own times, Ulrich Zwingli (1484-1531), one of the early leaders in the Protestant Reformation, called her "the ever chaste, immaculate Virgin Mary;" John Wesley (1703-1791), founder of the Methodist Church, extolled this extraordinary woman who continued after Christ's birth to be "a pure and unspotted virgin" (In his "Letter to a Roman Catholic"). No wonder in his sermon of September 1st, 1522, Martin Luther proclaimed that "The veneration of Mary is inscribed in the very depths of the human heart." Because her purity is without compare, surpassing all perfection of purity, Christian sages and mystics cannot find enough ways of describing what they know is beyond description. There is nothing lifeless about the images or symbols that hint at Mary's purity. This is because her purity is dancing with life and love, vaster than the ocean, more regular than a heartbeat, more gentle than a dewdrop, stronger than a cedar of Lebanon, whiter than a lily, purer than a pearl, more happy than a field of flowers, more sparkling than the stars, more fiery than the sun, more serene than a cloudless blue sky.

The rest of us are either impure or purified. To become purified is to become uncontaminated and undefiled. To be half-purified is to be impure, it is to be debased or corrupted. To become purified means to love with a love that is untainted by self-seeking. It means to have the glory of God as our only aim and sole intention. It means to be host to the pure desire of pleasing God. It means to refuse not only sin, but even to run away from the least infidelity to God. In other words, it is the most radical agenda possible. And it is possible because God invites us to full purification, not to half-measures. We can become like Jesus if we become all one with God.

But because we are human beings and sinners, our struggle against evil and sin is never finally resolved in this life. This is why it is more appropriate to talk of being purified rather than of being pure. We have not attained the goal of purity but find ourselves in the midst of incessant striving toward more and more purification. To participate in this striving means to attack the roots of evil within us, however flimsy and fragile they are. As Saint John of the Cross (1542-1591) pointed out, whether a bird is tied to the earth by a thread or a rope, it still cannot fly. The little things block our flight as much as the great, because they also bind us.

Purity is not a surface question, it is a core issue. It is not simply a matter of behavior; it is about who we are. Purity is not prudery and it is an awful pity to think about something as great as purity in such a childish way. Purity is on fire while prudery is cold as ice. Purity is passionate while prudery is frigid. Purity is animated and alive while prudery is deathly and repressed. Purity is attractive while prudery is a turn-off.

Purity is a burning question that touches the whole person. If we remain on the surface of the question, we can avoid ever facing its challenge and depth. It is easy to keep our distance from purity with cynicism and contempt. We can mock the naivety of those who are gullible enough to believe in it. And so we can refuse to get in touch with our own deepest hunger, which is for the fullness of life that purification promises.

How is purity attained? Are human willpower and motivation the crucial elements? In fact, as the country curate gradually came to realize in Georges Bernanos' classic novel *Diary of a Country Priest,* all is grace. It is all gratuitous love and unmerited favor. But on the other hand, we have to be generous in wanting good. We have to cooperate with God by exercising our free will. And although this often involves a struggle, it is always a graced struggle. Let's now explore this in more detail.

4

Running the Race

*Do you not know that in a race all the runners run,
but only one gets the prize? Run in such a way as to
get the prize.*

Saint Paul, First Letter to the Corinthians, 9:24

*Infinite striving to be the best is one's right. It is its
own reward. Everything else is in God's hands.*

Mahatma Gandhi, The Story of My Experiments with Truth

"We're on a mission from God," was the famous refrain of
the 1980 cult movie *The Blues Brothers*, a slapstick come-
dy of expensive stunts and endless car chases punctuated by
songs from some of the greatest soul and blues artists ever
— singers like Aretha Franklin, Ray Charles and James
Brown. Angels are on a mission from God. If you look
through the Bible you will find that angels are constantly
carrying out missions from God, whether it is the archangel
Michael and his angels battling the forces of evil on God's
behalf in Chapter 12 of the Book of Revelation, Gabriel
revealing to the Virgin Mary that Jesus is to be born to her
in the first chapter of Luke's Gospel, or Raphael telling

Tobit in Chapter 12 of the Book of Tobit that he has been sent by God to heal him from blindness and deliver his daughter-in-law Sarah from the demon afflicting her. To be available for mission the angels need to be focused on God and his plan; were they preoccupied with their own plans, they would not show instant readiness and availability. The success of angels is in their pure service of God, the single-ness of vision they constantly and admirably display. That is where we can emulate angelic purity. Obviously we cannot imitate angels by becoming spirits — we are not made that way. We are formed of body and soul, and we would be fleeing the human condition were we to try to renounce our material dimension. But while remaining the unique blend of body and soul that we are, we can nevertheless exist purely for God, focus our lives on him, and dedicate ourselves to his loving plan which is for the greatest good of each and everyone.

Something in us fears that God will demand too much of us; caution tells us to keep him at arm's length. Our lives could be so much happier if we did not follow such fears. The truth is that an indescribable joy awaits those who give themselves fully to God. We can't know how angels regard us, but let me make some conjectures. It is obvious to angels that God's mysterious plan is designed to bring extraordinary happiness to every human being. They know this plan can make an enormous and positive difference. But one thing that must perplex angels is how blasé we are about a God that guarantees us such happiness both now and in the next life. Angels must be stupefied by our coldness and hard-heartedness in the face of such love. On the one hand they rejoice in God's boundless love for human beings, a love without reservations or conditions. On the other hand, we are apparently indifferent to this love. The Creator of the universe, the Lord of all, shows awesome care for us, and yet we have the gall to go around ignoring it. We treat God as a stranger in the round of our normal lives, only calling upon him in dire emergencies. No wonder angels must seriously doubt our intelligence. Given the fact that those of us who believe in an afterlife are hoping to spend eternity in God's presence, angels must be astounded that we do not prepare by spending time in his presence now. If they did not know better, some of them would wonder if we had hearts at all.

Our tentative stance toward purity is rendered even more hesitant by the many fanciful tales going around about it. As a consequence, a lot of people don't even know what purity is. Moreover, they mistake purity for cheap counterfeits, and this is one of the reasons they could not be bothered about it. Popular consciousness often confuses purity with cringe-inducing dispositions like prudery and frigidity. More that that, Western culture often presents purity and sex as deadly enemies. But that is to misunderstand both sex and purity. Having absolutely no interest in sex does not automatically make persons pure; in fact, it makes them less than human. The truth is that the pure person reveres sex, and recognizes it as a great gift and a deep mystery. Even common sense tells us that without sex none of us would have been born in the first place. So if you're thinking, "purity would be great if I did not find sex so interesting," don't let that thought put you off, because the objection does not hold. Purity is not about forcing you to find sex repugnant or pretend it is uninteresting. Instead purity invites you to have a huge respect for sex. For the pure person, sex is like a temple, the kind of place you do not barge into but enter with awe and trepidation because you know you are in the presence of something sacred. And because sex is sacred, the pure person does not want to defile it by treating it in a frivolous or casual manner. It is a temple the pure person will only enter on the invitation of God.

The question of purity is not confined to the issue of sex. That is why the superficial understanding of purity needs to be deepened and the limited view of purity needs to be expanded. Too often we get bogged down in questions of detail about sexual morality, asking how far we may go and how much is permitted. These questions are childish and grown-ups ought to exhibit a more adult approach. Rather than becoming fixated by quantity, a qualitative approach is needed. The beauty of the Egyptian Pyramids is not because of the sheer quantity of stones but the quality of utter symmetry, harmony and proportion that strikes the observer. Purity is not a matter of rationally calculating how much we can safely afford to give. It is a question of giving as much as possible, pursuing perfection. It is the spirit of the firemen of 9-11 who did not ask how many flights of the World Trade Center it was safe to run up; they simply kept running because they were intent on saving human lives.

If we fix our eyes on the bigger picture and set ourselves the task of giving ourselves totally to God, then we automatically know there is no room for impurity and no space for lust. We recognize that purity is all-embracing. It brooks no compromises. And so we are immediately beyond lukewarm thoughts of half-measures and duplicity. Admittedly finding that kind of fullness is not an automatic discovery. We will make mistakes, we won't always get it right, we will often feel defeated by the weight of our humanity. But if our focus is on God, we will not be put off or disheartened by our own failures. If purity were something we had to achieve by ourselves alone, there would be more than enough reasons to be discouraged. But purity is a godly affair. If you are on your own and fall in the mud, you may be tempted to stay there. But if the one you love is next to you and reaches out a helping hand, it is much easier to get up. Pure persons entrust themselves to God. They are certain that he will lift them up. They know that he is totally reliable. He does not suffer mood swings; he does not change from one moment to the next. He possesses the most beautiful qualities imaginable with an undreamed of perfection. That is why pure persons find freedom by liberating themselves from their own egos. They stop seeking themselves, for to seek themselves is not to seek God. The pure only seek God. They know that to God alone belongs the glory. Since they do not yearn for their own glory, they are not ashamed when they fall. They are not even surprised, since they know they are human and not divine. They do not believe in their own divinity, and so they do not have to protect themselves. It is God's interests which they jealously guard. They have become "atheists" with regard to themselves. They know that there is one God who raises them up.

To be an undivided and devoted person we need to labor lovingly and be generously graced. Let's look at the loving labor first. In describing how to be a successful Christian, the Letter to the Hebrews uses language that evokes the Greek athletic games: "Let us throw off everything that hinders and the sin that so easily entangles, and let us run with perseverance the race marked out for us" (Hebrews 12:1). It is no wonder that examples from the Greek games are invoked on several occasions in the New

Testament (for instance also in 1 Corinthians 9:24-27 and 1 Timothy 4:8). The Olympic Games had been running for hundreds of years before the birth of Christ, and were still going strong during the first few hundred years of Christianity's existence. But more than the historical coincidence, there were and are many overt parallels between sports and the religious world. Like religion, sports taps into our human yearning for perfection, heroism, ritual, community, freedom within the context of clearly defined rules, and sacrifice in the cause of a noble goal. An unfortunate parallel between sports and religion is that many people enjoy discussing and watching both of them, but few really engage seriously in either.

Be that as it may, the Letter to the Hebrews invites its readers to cast off the weights, burdens and troubles that so easily bind and beset them. Probably in the back of the writer's mind was the common practice in Greek races of removing garments and sandals in order to be unencumbered and run faster. Long flowing robes looked well yet were anything but streamlined; sandals could easily break, causing the runner to fall and injure himself. Everything superfluous and necessary had to be shed for the duration of the race.

But long before they began to race competitively, athletes had to undergo a lengthy and strict training regimen. When athletes arrived at Olympia for the games, they had already been preparing for almost a year. In the weeks that followed, they adopted a more intensive program, eating a vegetarian diet, sleeping regularly, and being constantly monitored. If you are going to lose weight, you need motivation to carry you through the slimming program: you have to want it enough to make it happen. For a purifying diet you need motivation too: you must want to change enough to take the decisive action necessary.

The Greek runners were not only slowed down by the weight of their clothes; excess bodily weight also hindered them from peaking. For months before the Olympic Games they struggled to rid themselves of fat and flab, so that they could be fast enough to run. They ate what was good for the body, and abstained from harmful foods. They built up fitness and endurance. They developed skills and routines that became so ingrained and habitual that they no longer had to think about them. They could trust themselves to do what was needed at the time of competition without a moment's hesitation.

And yet this physical training was for a limited prize, not for a lasting and infinite reward: "For physical training is of some value, but godliness has value for all things, holding promise for both the present life and the life to come" (1 Timothy 4:8). Despite its limited scope, there is great value in reflecting upon athletic training and applying its lessons to Christian training:

> Do you not know that in a race all the runners run, but only one gets the prize? Run in such a way as to get the prize. Everyone who competes in the games goes into strict training. They do it to get a crown that will not last; but we do it to get a crown that will last forever. Therefore I do not run like a man running aimlessly; I do not fight like a man beating the air. No, I beat my body and make it my slave so that after I have preached to others, I myself will not be disqualified for the prize (1 Corinthians 9:24-27).

Paul talks about runners. When an athlete is about to start a race, it is vital to set aside distractions and to place his or her psychic and emotional focus on the race itself. For the brief time of the race, the whole being of the athlete needs to be focused on one thing only — running that race as fast as possible in order to win it. This singlemindedness is a form of purity. Such an undivided focus demands a tremendous expenditure of energy — physical and spiritual; Christianity too demands the pure commitment of the whole human being. In order to get the prize, the runner needs to move in a forward direction and keep focused on the finishing line; looking around and running sideways is a sure way to lose the race. Runners are so intent on winning that they discount the pain involved in view of the prize ahead. Some run through the pain barrier, and indeed it seems from empirical studies that physical exercise increases the pain threshold. Even daily joggers, although wary of pain, are more than willing to endure discomfort and to make sacrifices, such as getting out of a warm bed to run in the cold morning when staying inside is more enticing, and forgoing sedentary lifestyles and high-cholesterol diets in order to maintain physical fitness.

Runners have clearly-defined goals. A goal is something that we want to attain or achieve. Those who want to run the Christian race need clarity about the goal of this race. Without clear goals, it is difficult to make clear progress. Vague goals often lead nowhere or down blind alleys. The goal of Christianity is clear and simple, both in the immediate future and in the long-term: to seek God, to know God and to love God with every fiber of one's being. Christianity is not about half-measures or watered-down compromises. It calls for the purity of complete commitment. The successful pursuit of this goal leads to the happiness of being with God forever in paradise.

A definite future goal helps in the articulation of present decisions that work towards the goal. A sure goal gives direction to life. A certain goal gathers and guides energy that would otherwise be dispersed and diminished, enabling the person to distinguish what is significant from what is of little importance. To become a goal, something needs to be explicitly articulated by the person. It needs to be remembered, mulled over, sung, painted, written down, dreamed about. The goal has to become so concrete and real that it is as though we can reach out and touch it, hold it, and taste it. Only then can we become passionate and motivated.

But for all this talk of our effort, it is nevertheless impossible to persevere in the race of love without God's help. It is not easy always to think, speak and act as Jesus would, or do all the little things of life in union with him. Total trust in God does not come naturally. It is not a matter of course to use every moment of time for God's glory and the good of others. It is difficult to refrain from judging people. It is tempting to forget to converse with God and instead to neglect prayer.

We need to ask God's help; and to boost our confidence in God, we need to open our eyes to how God is already helping us. If we reflect upon our lives, we can quickly see that there have been many times when we have been unexpectedly preserved from danger — the car that should have run us down when we blindly dashed across a busy street, but amazingly missed us; the tackle on the football field that was strong enough to break our leg but didn't. There have been many times when people have surprisingly appeared to help us on our journey: the kind woman who went out of her way to help us find our camping site in a foreign country, the colleague who unknowingly spoke words that touched us profoundly, the singer whose song helped us surmount an emotional crisis. These were not coincidences; they were "God-incidences." It was God who was working through these people and situations to guard us and guide us.

But if we insist on doing everything ourselves, how can God help us, and without him at our side how can we realistically expect to succeed in the race? If we want to see the miraculous help of God in our lives, we must ask him to assist us and trust that he will. Since he managed to create the world and continues to keep it in being, surely it would not be too much for him to provide for us? If we rely exclusively on ourselves, we will become worse versions of ourselves. If we rely on God, we will become the best versions of ourselves. Even if the goal of pure love seems unrealistic and impossible, with God everything is possible.

The question we are left with is the question posed by the Florentine-born Saint Philip Neri (1515-1595), who became known as the apostle of Rome. It was a question he used ask to awaken faith, hope and love — "When shall we begin to do good?"

5

The Big Picture: Good Versus Evil

*And there was a war in heaven. Michael and his
angels fought against the dragon, and the dragon
and his angels fought back. But he was not strong
enough, and they lost their place in heaven. The
great dragon was hurled down — the ancient serpent called the devil, or Satan, who leads the whole
world astray. He was hurled to the earth, and his
angels with him.*

The Book of Revelation 12:7-9

*This is the way, I suppose, that the world will be
destroyed — amid the universal hilarity of wits and
wags who think it is all a joke.*

Søren Kierkegaard, *Either-Or*, Volume 1

In this chapter I am going to talk about evil, Satan, demons,
the battle for the soul, and how cleanliness is not next to
godliness. But first I want to share a haunting parable from
Søren Kierkegaard (1813-1855), whom the twentieth century philosopher Ludwig Wittgenstein called "by far the most
profound thinker of the last [nineteenth] century."

On February 20th, 1843, the book *Either-Or* was published in Copenhagen, Denmark. True to its title, this book, published in two volumes, was about choice. The first volume, "either," effortlessly depicted an amoral view of existence. The second volume, "or," dutifully laid out the virtues of a moral way of life. And just to confuse readers who thought they were being confronted with a choice between these alternatives, the book ended with a sermon, suggesting that faith was the real goal. To complicate matters even more, the author of this brilliant and infuriating book, Søren Kierkegaard, went to elaborate lengths to conceal the fact that he wrote it, using a go-between to deliver the manuscript to the printer, even though his authorship quickly became the best known secret in Copenhagen. Instead of putting his own name on the front cover, Kierkegaard invented a fictitious editor for *Either-Or* with the mystifying Latin name Victor Eremita, which means "Victorious Hermit" or "Triumphant Solitary." Perhaps Kierkegaard chose this monastic name because he was intent on leading a more cloistered life in the wake of his highly-publicized break-up with one of the most beautiful women of Copenhagen, Regine Olsen. Maybe Kierkegaard also had in mind the solitary existence that the process of writing necessarily imposes. But there was no danger that the public would associate Kierkegaard's lifestyle with the solitude of a monk. During the period when he was correcting the proofs of *Either-Or*, he made a point of dropping into the theater each evening for precisely ten minutes. He knew that the town gossips would spread the word that he spent all his evenings there. But after his statutory ten minutes were up, Kierkegaard would immediately rush home and release his cascading thoughts onto paper, often staying up long into the night.

In the preface to *Either-Or*, the "Victorious Hermit" tells the convoluted story of how he came into possession of the papers that make up the book. He bought a writing desk that caught his eye in a secondhand shop. Some time later, being unable to open the money drawer, he hit the desk with a hatchet and a secret door he had never noticed before suddenly sprang open. Inside he found two voluminous groups of papers. The first group of papers forms the first volume of *Either-Or*, supposedly written by someone called "A," a romantic figure with a devil-may-care attitude to life, the incarnation of Kierkegaard's famous aesthetic stage, or pleasure-loving phase of life. This set of papers begins with a number of short vignettes. Most of them have a moral to tell. Indeed at certain moments "A" reminds us of the serious Kierkegaard behind the superficial public face, for despite the fact that "A" is meant to be a carefree and flippant character, he is prone to make profound and pithy observations.

One of the most memorable is the following harrowing parable: it happened that a fire broke out offstage in a theater. In desperation the clown, all dressed up in his costume, ran on stage to instruct the audience to leave the theater at once. But the audience mistook the clown's warning for his act and applauded. The more he warned them and the more wildly he gesticulated, the more heartily they laughed, until the whole theater was engulfed in flames. In like manner, "A" gleefully comments, the world will end in general applause from the wits, who think it is a joke.

I do not think the world is about to end — yet. But I wonder if we, like the complacent audience in that imaginary theater, aren't deceived about our true predicament. We nod in assent when contemporary prophets warn of the evils of consumerism and happily continue consuming to excess. We respectfully listen to the dire predictions of massive climate change and calmly live with constantly rising levels of carbon dioxide emissions. We feel that the sexualization of Western culture has gone too far, yet do nothing to counter the precocious sexualization of our children. Pope Benedict XVI eloquently observed in his inaugural sermon of April 24, 2005 that "the external deserts in the world are growing, because the internal deserts have become so vast."

Sometimes we feel there is little we can do. The idols of money, power and sex are omnipresent and elusive, not centered in any one place, but extending everywhere, like an evil empire without boundaries whose power percolates through the whole planet. Some people mistakenly shoulder all the blame for our ills on globalization or the U.S. or Islamic militants or many other predictable scapegoats. Christianity comes up with another cause, one that can be expressed in a single word. The word is "evil." This word seems too simple, yet evil itself is mystifying: it is the mystery of iniquity. We find evil all around us and we cannot pin it down: it eludes and baffles us. Evil is an immense question that threatens to defeat human understanding. It is difficult to throw a lot of light on something that is essentially dark. The best answer to give to someone suffering from evil is not a theoretical answer, but the answer of concrete love. In the world of experience, it is only by receiving the victorious love of Jesus Christ that a person can escape the clutches of evil. Ultimately, human reason cannot cope with the mystery of evil; only God can overcome it. From the point of view of our own welfare, we instinctively prefer neither to encounter nor endure evil. We really experience it, yet we find it to be something that impoverishes rather than enriches us, depriving us of what we need for a full human life.

Evil is the lack of something that should be there: it is the privation of a good thing. Sight is absent in a flower and in a blind person, but its absence in the case of the flower is not a privation because a flower was never meant to see in the first place. Blindness is only attributed to beings that were born to see. We do not say that a human being suffers from the privation of wings, as though he or she were meant to have them. We simply say that human beings are without wings. The capacity to fly is not part of human nature, though the capacity to see is. Blindness is not a complete reality. Instead it is the lack of something that should be present in the organ of the eye.

Evil is not a thing in itself, it is the privation of something, just as darkness is not a thing in itself but the lack of light waves. If there were no light, we would not be talking of darkness, but of nothing. A hole in a sock is not a thing in itself, but only exists as a hole in the context of the sock. A hole in a sock robs the sock of its completeness. Evil is parasitical in the sense that it does not exist of itself, but only as the corruption of something good. Something cannot be totally evil, in other words totally lacking in something, because if the good were totally annihilated, evil would no longer be able to exist either: if a sock were truly full of holes, there would be no sock, and so there would be no holes, simply nothing. If there were no good things, there could be no evil, because there would be nothing for evil to inhere in.

A helpful analogy for evil is the virus, this ultramicroscopic agent that invades healthy cells of living things, finding conditions in which to thrive and replicate. A virus requires a living organism in order to reproduce and multiply, just as evil only exists in a thing. A virus is a thing, evil is not; yet a virus is similar to evil since it is on the border between being and nothingness: of itself a virus is inert and can only replicate within living host cells. Indeed there is debate about whether a virus is a living or non-living agent. Because viruses are invisible under the best light microscopes, virologists observe them in an indirect manner, through observing the host cell in which they lodge. Evil is observed through how it corrupts things. Evil is a parasitic and corrupting influence. God's creation is characterized by order. Evil, like the virus, introduces disorder into living beings.

Just as the virus is and is not a living agent, it is as though evil does and does not exist. Evil does not exist to the extent that it is not a positive reality — evil is a privation. But evil exists as a privation, just as blindness exists as the lack of something that ought to be there. Evil, like sickness, exists, but not as a thing. Sickness exists as the lack of something — health — that should be present. Evil exists as the lack of the goodness that should be. Although evil is not a real thing, it really affects us in life: we suffer because of others and ourselves, and because of the world we live in. Evil is not powerless and it is not an illusion. There is nothing impotent or illusory about the physical evil of an earthquake or the moral evil of being mugged. Evil can have devastating consequences: whether the AIDS virus is or is not a living agent, it has destroyed millions of lives. Therefore we conceive of evil as real, as the real dissonance or disparity with the goodness that should be present. In fact, the greater the goodness in which evil parasitically lodges, the more mayhem it can lead to. That is why the evil of someone who has more good capacities (because of natural endowment, education, and so on) is much more devastating and "real" than the evil of someone who has few talents. For instance, an evil nuclear physicist of genius could use his or her intelligence to cause worldwide destruction, whereas a person without education could at most inflict such destruction accidentally; an evil religious leader of great charisma could lead innumerable people to ruin, whereas an evil member of a local congregation without any personal radiance or leadership qualities could not wreak such havoc unaided.

Let me elaborate more on this insight, and first of all please forgive me if your pearl necklace or gold wristwatch has been lifted recently, because I am about to take the goodness of jewelry thieves as an example. Of course stealing jewelry is wrong: there is no doubt that jewelry thieves carry out morally bad actions. But in order to do so, they employ qualities that are good in themselves. They deploy patience (for a bad purpose), planning a heist for months in advance. They display perseverance, going to enormous trouble to obtain the phone numbers and personal data of their intended targets, and painstakingly check their routes to and from work. They show a penetrating intelligence, realizing that all sorts of equipment, from lock picks to eavesdropping bugs, from fake mustaches to bulletproof vests, may prove necessary. When perpetrating the crime, they can exhibit surprising creativity, finding unexpected aid in the most mundane items like bubblegum, which they have been known to spread on their palms so that the diamonds they touch remain firmly stuck there. They are happy to hire buxom blondes in order to distract the attention of male employees in jewelry stores.

Surprising as it seems, the evil committed by jewelry thieves depends for its success on faculties which in themselves are good. To put it another way, an impatient, irresolute, slow-witted and unimaginative jewelry thief will not be good at being evil. It is as though evil "piggy backs" on these good qualities. Furthermore, when someone chooses to steal jewelry, that person does it because he or she perceives some good in it. Now this good is patently not of the same level as the good sought by Francis of Assisi: saints are distinguished by choosing the eternal good — God — in all their actions. Rather this good is a particular good — for instance, a jewelry thief sees the good of having enough money to pay off the bills, buy a condominium, and take a dream vacation. However, in this specific situation of robbery, the jewelry thief chooses this particular good in defiance of the much greater good of respecting the divine commandment, "Thou shalt not steal," and so the limited good he seeks for himself is accompanied by a lot of evil. It is important to stress that God's commandment is not a cold moral imperative or an obligation imposed from without, but the interior exigency of human nature. In other words the human being has an obligation to his or her own nature, which is simultaneously an obligation to God. The enlightened conscience and God's commandments speaks similar words to human beings.

If the example of jewelry thieves seems too remote, let us take one closer to home. Although Christians ideally seek the good, they also confess responsibility for the worst crime of all time. The most abominable act of moral evil ever committed in history was the murder of the Son of God. It is bad enough to consider killing a human being, but to want to kill God is infinitely worse. Christians accept that they, along with the rest of humankind, are the cause of this awful deed. Were it not for their sins, Jesus would not have been condemned to such a horrendous death. Now all Christians would also agree that the goal of their actions has not been and is not the perpetration of this awful act of killing Jesus Christ; yet at the same time, they readily admit that despite their good will and because of their fragility, their sins contribute to the death of Jesus. Nevertheless, in doing morally bad things they are seeking goals they perceive as good; they are not consciously seeking to kill the Second Person of the Blessed Trinity.

The human will is attracted to what the person understands to be good. This optimistic view is not a new discovery, but enjoys a long tradition. The Greek philosopher Aristotle (384-322 BC) begins his *Nicomachean Ethics* by asserting that the good is what everyone seeks. This is not to deny that Christians are aware they are doing wrong by committing morally evil acts. Despite their awareness of doing wrong, at the moment they sin they substitute the eternal good of God with a lesser good which is irrelevant or illusory and conflicts against the greater good in that particular situation. A classic example is Eve in the Garden of Eden: she notices that the fruit is pleasant to eat and erroneously believes it will make her like God, but she chooses to ignore a vastly more significant good with which this particular good conflicts: the importance of obeying God's command which resounds within her heart. Therefore, in sinning, Christians "miss the mark" (the Greek word mostly used for sin in the New Testament comes from archery, and means precisely this: "to miss the mark"), pursuing the wrong goals and falling short of the right objectives, by committing morally bad acts which go against the commandments of God and the interior law of their own nature. However, it is not the evil that attracts their wills, but the good.

Because the will is naturally oriented to the good, a person doing what is morally bad is invariably seeking the good. Of course this does not mean that the person cannot be held accountable for what they wrongly do. The person is responsible for any morally bad act that is freely chosen. Indeed the Roman Catholic Church teaches that sins which have grave matter as their object (for example killing, committing adultery, stealing, and so on), and which are committed with full knowledge of the sinful nature of the deed allied to deliberate and free consent to it, destroy love in the human heart. Because of this murderous effect, these sins are known as mortal sins.

The evil of some persons in history strikes us as so complete that it seems they have chosen evil for its own sake. They have descended to such a depth of evil that evil has become their good, even though evil in fact is the complete absence or privation of goodness. This demonic tendency is well illustrated in the epic poem *Paradise Lost* by John Milton (1608-1674), where Satan creates a perverse reversal of values, freely deciding that he will always conceive of evil as good: "Evil, be thou my good." Milton's Satan persuades himself that his evil is not evil at all. Satan apes God in a devilish way by making evil his good out of hatred for God's true goodness. Of course the fact that Satan decides evil is good does not make it good. It does, however, confirm him as an inveterate liar. One wonders if the devil's deceit blinded even Milton, who made Satan so much more appealing than God in *Paradise Lost.*

Everything that God made is good, so evil does not originate from the Creator. "God saw all that he had made, and it was very good" (Genesis 1:31). Everything that exists has at least the goodness of simply "being." It is good to be. Evil uses this good to spread itself. According to the Christian tradition, evil originated in Lucifer, the most beautiful angel of all, inferior only to God in majesty. Had Lucifer possessed less good qualities to start with, he would not have become so effective at being evil. Because at first he shone so brightly, he entered the darkness more deeply when he fell. Lucifer, whose name means "light-bearer," fell like lightning from heaven (see Luke 10:18), changing into a creature of darkness. Perhaps evil arose in Lucifer like a virus can in a perfectly healthy body, initially invading his spirit like a practically invisible infection, a particle of pride that led him to attribute his beauty and greatness to himself rather than to God. He helped nourish this derailing virus of pride by dwelling on it and believing it so much that he tried to usurp God with the help of myriad other rebel angels. Their rebellion was a totally free act; it was accomplished by proud spirits of perfect intelligence who were fully aware of the consequences and who, even were it possible, would never go back on this fateful choice.

The abyss of evil is always in proportion to the height and goodness of the being it devastates. In other words, the greater the good of the being in which evil thrives, the worse the evil that will result. This is why Lucifer, the angel who was originally the summit of created goodness, became evil in an utterly harrowing sense of the term once he fell. The whole power of his being, which was previously devoted solely to goodness, afterwards became exclusively directed towards evil. And yet, since evil preys on and destroys goodness, if Satan were fully evil he would no longer exist since there would be no goodness, however diminished and debased, within which evil could thrive. This point was expressed with eloquent simplicity by a saintly Irishwoman, who never had a bad word to say about anyone. One day, to test her, someone asked her what she thought of the devil. "In all fairness to him," she replied, "he never stops working." Satan works tirelessly for evil.

The fallen angels are called demons and ceaselessly wander the earth tempting human beings to do evil. Thrown out of heaven by the archangel Michael (the meaning of whose name — "who is like God?" — signifies humility), Satan and his demons seek revenge on God by seducing human beings to evil. Their intelligence is far superior to that of humans and they are adept at pinpointing character failings and exploiting them. But they have no power to harm the human soul unless human beings freely invite them in.

You may have already noticed that in the course of this book I sometimes mention Satan, otherwise known as the devil, the leader of the rebel angels called demons. But I refer to him in a matter of fact way, because even though the devil exists, it is wise not to get melodramatic in the face of this reality. Otherwise we run the risk of attributing too much importance to him and becoming excessively fearful. Satan's power is limited: he is only a creature, not God. As a rule, it is best not to become too interested in Satan, if we do not want to run the risk of being poisoned by his venom. And besides, curiosity is healthy only when it is a desire to know the good. Morbid or contaminating curiosity is unhealthy and inappropriate: it is the drive to know things that are evil, or to become acquainted with the occult. This kind of curiosity corrupts and even destroys the curious person. The pure person seeks God, and avoids what is not God. The pure person recognizes that there are evil influences at work in our world, but does not want to know the sources of evil. The pure person seeks God whole-heartedly, and so there is none of the heart left for anything base.

I interchangeably use the terms Satan, the devil, the demon and the evil spirit when I refer to what tempts us to evil, because evil originates in the devil. But it is not always Satan who entices us to evil: other fallen angels can do so, as can the false values in our cultures, or the unhealthy dispositions within ourselves. So although I refer to one or other of the names for Satan, my intention is also to include all these other forces that act against God's love in our lives. None of these factors that conspire against goodness compel us to do evil; they certainly propose and suggest it. But it is we ourselves who take the initiative in falling away from love.

While exaggerated interest in Satan is imprudent, it is also unwise to dismiss the idea of the devil or deny his existence as a flight of fancy or superstition. People who do not believe in viruses end up taking unnecessary risks and pay the price. Satan exists. He is not just present in out-of-the-ordinary phenomena like cases of possession; he is not only to be found in Satanic cults. Of course he is not always readily apparent since deceit is his trademark. It is evident from the serpent's temptation of Eve in Genesis that Satan's main strategy to get inside human beings is through the gateway of the senses — Eve *sees* attractive fruit and relishes the prospect of *tasting* and eating it.

In a famous address of November 15, 1972, Pope Paul VI pointed out that Satan is not part of some big and remote cosmic scenario that has nothing to do with us; rather his presence intrudes wherever there is evil:

> We can presume that his sinister action is at work where the denial of God becomes radical, subtle and absurd; where lies become powerful and hypocritical in the face of evident truth; where love is smothered by cold, cruel selfishness; where Christ's name is attacked with conscious, rebellious hatred; where the spirit of the Gospel is watered down and rejected; where despair is affirmed as the last word . . .

The little picture is the tapestry of our everyday lives, made up largely of small struggles and joys, of choices that we often barely reflect on. The big picture is more dramatic: on one side there is God with his angels, nourishing faith, hope and love in human beings; on the other side there is Satan with all his demons, inciting human beings towards hatred, despair and atheism. The battlefield is the human soul. We are in a war zone. But the spiritual struggle is not like a human war, which sooner or later becomes demonic in its murderous rage. Human war is characterized by violence and leads to the bitterness of hate, the cold poison of resentment, and the consuming thirst for revenge. Christians renounce evil weapons and hateful armor. They put on faith, hope and love as their weapons in spiritual combat, confident that these arms guarantee victory. The odds are more than stacked on the side of goodness because the power of light is infinitely superior to the power of darkness, and victory is assured, if only human beings want it. The little picture that is the individual struggle to be good is a vital part of the big picture: the seemingly inconsequential moral choices of daily life are hugely significant, because through them each person can become part of the love that is in the process of transfiguring the universe.

The definitive victory of good over evil will only become clear at the end of time. Only then will it become evident that God has permitted evil, not only out of respect for human freedom but also and especially because he has the mysterious and awesome ability to draw goodness out of evil, despite the ravages of sin. The evil of sin leads to disaster, yet God is able transform all things, even such catastrophe, to the good. But this does not mean that sin brings about good; only God can do that. Evil can never of itself lead to goodness; it can never cause love.

God permits moral evil, but he by no means causes it. In fact, God abhors the evil of sin. To say that God permits such evil does not mean he condones it or approves of it. What God does approve of and respect is human freedom, and it is because he cherishes freedom so highly that he suffers sin. And God does indeed suffer sin: in Jesus Christ, God made man, he suffered it to an outrageous extent, to the point of a horrific death. Sin hurt the Word of God to the extent of killing him. Sin hurts the love of God. Sin was never God's invention. Whether evil takes the form of physical suffering or the moral evil of sin, it is abhorrent. Without denying its repulsive character, God can bring greater good out of it. Of course, in the darkness of suffering, this greater goodness is not visible. In the present, the followers of Christ shed tears at the evil of the world, reach out to help those who suffer, pray for them, and hope despite all evidence to the contrary, that love is the final and victorious word. God asks them to trust the light in the midst of the greatest darkness, to say a life-affirming yes when all around the voices of negation threaten to drown out their loving cries.

In the context of the big picture, pure love is vital. Why? There is already a hidden answer in the birth of Jesus. Christians believe that when the Son of God, through whom the whole universe was created, lowered himself to become a human being, he was born in a stable used to house animals. His crib was a manger, an animal feeding trough. Our romanticized Christmas cribs do not reproduce the dung, dirt, cobwebs and unpleasant smell that would have greeted the Son of God in this enclosed space. Some Christians no doubt find the very idea of God being born in such surroundings utterly repugnant: the picture simply does not harmonize with their rightfully exalted image of God. Why would the Father, whose care is so focused that he even knows the number of hairs on our head, have allowed this? Was he not providing for his only Son? Come to think of it, why did his perfect plan allow the heavily pregnant Mary make a four day journey from Nazareth to Bethlehem and then vainly seek for shelter in this little town before finding the manger?

Obviously the Son of God was willing to accept dust and dirt. Unlike the 20th century American billionaire Howard Hughes (1905-1976), Jesus was not obsessed with physical cleanliness; he did not have a phobia about germs. Although a popular saying proclaims that "cleanliness is next to Godliness," this is untrue: "Don't you see that nothing that enters a man from the outside can make him unclean?" (Mark 7:18) The cleanliness that counts has

nothing to do with externals, with outward rituals and cere-
monies. Instead it is a matter of the heart: "What comes out
of a man is what makes him unclean" (Mark 7:20). Hygiene
is not the same as holiness and excessive concern about the
former can lead us away from the latter, as the following
tragic and true story illustrates.

On the morning of February 18, 1943, almost a hundred
years to the day after Kierkegaard's *Either-Or* was published, the brother and sister Hans and Sophie Scholl, both
students at the University of Munich, arrived at college with
a suitcase full of anti-Nazi pamphlets. They belonged to a
student resistance group with the beautifully pure name
"The White Rose." While lectures were in session and the
halls deserted, they distributed the pamphlets by stacking
them outside doors, on staircases and upon window sills.
When they had finished distributing the pamphlets, Hans
and Sophie realized that the suitcase was not quite empty so
they scooped out the remaining ones and threw them from
the highest floor down into the courtyard below. Hans and
Sophie were seen by the janitor, Jakob Schmid, who immediately had them arrested. Four days later Hans and Sophie
were executed. The most encouraging aspect of that
February morning was the courageous stand of these young
Germans. The most astounding aspect of that morning was
the janitor's motivation for reporting Hans and Sophie to
the authorities. He later insisted it had nothing to do with
their action being a call to resistance or an act of treason
against this unjust state. Schmid was indignant and upset for
an entirely different reason: the two students had dirtied the
courtyard he was entrusted to keep clean. Order and cleanliness were his priorities, and he claimed afterwards that he

would have acted the same no matter what kind of paper had been scattered on the ground.

Cleanliness and order should not be discounted, but they pale into insignificance when compared to the value of a human life. The janitor put something insignificant in the place of what was really important. He gave an idolatrous centrality to physical cleanliness. This disordered reversal, where the body usurps the place of the soul, is not a new phenomenon. Jesus accused some Pharisees of his time of being whitewashed tombs, "whited sepulchres" (Matthew 23:27), handsome on the outside, but full of stinking bones inside. They appeared sumptuous in all their finery, yet their hearts were defiled. Fellow human beings noticed their external appearance and saw their outward actions; Jesus discerned their inner intent and spiritual corruption.

Unlike the janitor at the University of Munich, Jesus was not upset at the lack of cleanliness and order in the Bethlehem stable. Yet the Second Person of the Blessed Trinity was adamant about one thing: there had to be interior cleanliness in the woman who bore him. As Son of the Most High God, he himself is holiness, the purity of love, and he wanted to see the purity of heaven mirrored in the pure love of the woman who bore him. Only someone pure could dare to hold and touch the Pure One. Because he was held by a woman who radiated the sweet and unsullied scent of sanctity, the dirt of the stable did not ruffle him. Mary was pure. As Martin Luther (1483-1546) proclaimed in his sermon "On the Day of the Conception of the Mother of God" from 1527:

It is a sweet and pious belief that the infusion of Mary's soul was effected without original sin; so that in the very infusion of her soul she was also purified from original sin and adorned with God's gifts, receiving a pure soul infused by God; thus from the first moment she began to live she was free from all sin.

When the Word of God chose to be born of Mary, he chose joy. A pure person is a person of profound joy. Unfortunately many people instinctively equate virtue with difficulty, and presume that the measure of moral greatness is the intensity of pain that accompanies it. When taken to an extreme, this attitude leads to mistrust and hostility in the face of joy. Sadly, one of the factors that attracts people to impurity is the promise of a pleasure they believe cannot be found in purity. For the truth is that human beings are created to be happy, and if they do not find it where they ought to — in the realm of faith — they will look for it where it is not truly to be found.

Another reason for confusion between purity and impurity is that "desire" is a key term in each. However, there is a crucial difference: lust is the excessive desire for something destructive, whereas purity is the immense yearning for someone infinitely good. Someone once compared lust to the craving for salt by someone who is dying of thirst in the desert. In other words, lust is a recipe for spiritual suicide. Purity is the craving for living water by someone who is parched in the desert: it is the longing for abundant life.

Just like Satan in his envy continually tries to imitate God and only succeeds in copying the Almighty in a distorted fashion, so vices tend to be hellish imitations of the corresponding virtues, and that is why lust is illicit desire

through which persons lose self-control and throw themselves away, whereas purity is healthy desire by which persons become more themselves than ever before and carry
themselves upward.

Love and sex are not the same. The sexual urge, which
is instinctive, can give rise to strong desires for another person. But without respect and understanding, and without
mutual commitment, there is no love, only strong sexual
feelings. The sexual urge is not rational, and so the man
dominated by it ignores the fact that he could destroy the
happy marriage of the stunning woman he meets at a dinner
party. His sexual instinct is only affected by her extraordinary beauty.

The figure we are about to look at in the next chapter is
unashamedly libidinous, and one of the most undeveloped
human beings ever depicted in music, because he gives a
completely free rein to his instincts. These urges completely dominate his life. But despite his infantile nature, many
men are downright envious of him and his conquests. He is
a man who neither knows how to love or be loved, yet he
knows exactly what he desires, and what he desires is not
just one woman but every woman. He is one of the most
seductive incarnations of the Don Juan myth. His songs are
enchanting, but then not all songs are worth singing.

6

The Seductive Singer

When the daughter of Herodias came in and danced,
she pleased Herod and his dinner guests.

Mark 6:22

Was that a high C, or Vitamin D?

Groucho Marx, *A Night at the Opera*

A Night at the Opera was one of the most successful Marx Brothers' films ever made, not only because of the zany gags, anarchic humor, and even the presence of a loose storyline, but also because the Marx madness mocked the self-importance and stuffiness of grand opera. Unfortunately, opera continues to have an elitist label, conjuring up pictures of plush seats, portly singers and protuberant wallets. Some people wonder how anybody could endure an art form in which a soprano sings her undying love in an aria that lasts five long minutes, periodically hitting uncomfortably high notes that make her voice sound like a stainless steel knife mercilessly scratching an enamel plate.

That is why the opera *Don Giovanni* by Wolfgang Amadeus Mozart (1756-1791) is so refreshing. Despite being over two hundred years old, it still comes across as a breath of fresh air that blows the stuffiness out of opera. It is lusciously alive, seething with energy; it soars skyward with unforgettable melodies. Søren Kierkegaard said of the opera what the protagonist's jilted lover Elvira said of him: "You have destroyed my happiness," because it took such a hold upon the Danish philosopher, expelling him from the serenity of a cloistered existence, that he was unable and unwilling to forget it. The story is primarily comic, with moments of tragedy that become inflated to gargantuan proportions at the end. In a departure from tradition, Mozart did not name the opera after an exemplar of virtue or a wronged man or one who won integrity through suffering, but after someone who is not intended as a role model at all — the recklessly amoral and dissolute Don Giovanni, who sees women as prey rather than persons. Despite his undeniable charm, the Don is a heartless killer. The opening scene of the opera is marked by his murder of an old man, the Commendatore. Having tormented the Commendatore's daughter inside her father's house before the curtains open — the opera never makes clear whether Don Giovanni seduces the girl or rapes her — the Don flees, and Donna Anna's screams awaken her father. The Commendatore emerges and challenges Don Giovanni to a duel. The Don kills the elderly man, and promptly flees the scene of the crime in the company of his manservant Leporello. Donna Anna vows revenge, but in the end it is the stone statue of the Commendatore himself that comes to life and drags Don Giovanni down to hellfire and damnation. Don Giovanni's licentious life ultimately destroys him. Given his brutality and callousness, why name an opera after such a self-centered and ruthless cad? Perhaps to show how devilishly alluring evil can be, because make no mistake about it, Don Giovanni is the most fascinating and entrancing character in the whole opera. The subtitle of Mozart's opera is *"dramma giocoso,"* which can be translated as "playful drama". For the most part the script suggests a comic aim. But there is certainly nothing playful about the ending of the opera, when Don Giovanni is consigned to hellfire. Having committed murder and repeatedly seduced and deceived without showing the least qualms of conscience or inclination to change his ways, the punishment seems apt, but for the fact that the Don is so infantile that he does not have a conscience. Indeed his character seems too insubstantial to be a real human being. Nevertheless his rollercoaster trip to damnation sweeps listeners off their feet with the same winning charm that his manservant Leporello assures us works so well with women.

The Don Juan character first emerged in literary form in the play *El Burlador de Sevilla y Convidado de Pietra*, written in 1630 by the Spanish monk Gabriel Tellez, more commonly known as Tirso de Molina. This Don Juan figure was a more serious and sinister creation than later versions. Although he was happy to make fun of other people, he did not tolerate the least affront to his own sense of superiority and would fight to the death to defend his so-called "honor." He was not an atheist, yet he refused to bow before the supernatural. He used women with reckless abandon because he felt it was his inborn right to do so. Despite his brutality, there was gravity and even nobility in Tirso de Molina's Don Juan. These were not enough to save him but they did elevate his fate to the level of tragedy. Although rightfully cast into hell, Don Juan embodied a tragic grandeur, which is another way of saying that Tirso de Molina was a gifted dramatist. When the legend of Don Juan spread to Italy, it changed significantly in character. The Italians transformed him into a figure of farce, a comical buffoon; they exaggerated his seductive streak and his arrogance to such an extent that he no longer seemed a human being. This was also to be the case for Lorenzo Da Ponte (1749-1853), who wrote the Italian libretto for Mozart's *Don Giovanni*, and also for *The Marriage of Figaro* and *Così Fan Tutte*.

"She speaks like a novel," Don Giovanni's servant Leporello wittily comments after a hysterical outburst of the Don's jilted lover Donna Elvira. Da Ponte, who wrote these words and all the other lyrics in *Don Giovanni*, had a life that was more eventful than most novels. Born into a Jewish family in 1749 in a town about 40 miles north of Venice, Lorenzo Da Ponte's real name was Emanuele Conegliano. But in order to facilitate the marriage of his father, a widower, to a young Catholic woman, he converted to Catholicism as a boy of 14 along with his two brothers, taking the name and surname of the bishop who baptized him: Lorenzo Da Ponte. Blessed with a prodigious memory and a lively intelligence, Lorenzo became a student in the best educational institution of his local town of Ceneda (now known as Vittorio Veneto): the seminary.

In 1773 Da Ponte was ordained a priest, a ministry he never exercised, and moved to Venice, where he became tutor in an aristocratic family. He relished his new-found freedom in Venice and the opportunity to fulfill his literary ambitions. He also spent most of his free time gambling and womanizing. Almost inevitably he lost his position, moving to the nearby town of Treviso. Here he briefly taught Latin and rhetoric at the local seminary, before being expelled from his teaching post for avant-garde views. He once again returned to Venice, taking up the post of private tutor in a different household. But soon his new employer was arrested for radical political ideas and Da Ponte was accused of having a concubine. Now 30 years of age, Da Ponte was banned from Venice and its territories for the next 15 years.

Having spent a couple of fruitless years looking for work as a librettist in places like Dresden, Da Ponte made his way to Vienna in 1781 where he was to enjoy the most productive period of his life, putting his literary gifts to good use by collaborating with the greatest composers at the court of the Emperor Joseph II, among whom were Salieri and of course Mozart. Joseph II himself played the viola and cello, and took a hands-on interest in music. When Joseph II decided to restore the Italian opera theater in 1782, Da Ponte was made the poet of the theater. His task was not to write pure poetry, but musical lyrics that would be both poetic (that is, imaginatively articulated, rich in images, and capturing the melody of language) and dramatic (with the emphasis on entertainment and moving the action along in an engaging manner). Da Ponte was soon happily inundated with work, with the result that Mozart was put on the waiting list. In a letter to his father from 1783 Mozart wrote that Da Ponte had promised to write a libretto for him once he had completed work for Salieri, but added that Da Ponte's pledge was given with that dubious Italian charm that promises much only perhaps to deliver little.

It was during his time in Vienna that Da Ponte became a close friend of the legendary lover, Giacomo Casanova. In 1785 Casanova, then 60 years of age, was living in Vienna, and working as the secretary of the Venetian Ambassador. Practically every day he went for long walks with his younger friend Da Ponte, who was 36. As well as hailing from the same region of Italy, Casanova and Da Ponte shared a consuming passion for gambling and above all women, and had a sublime disregard for financial constraints, spending money as if there were no tomorrow. In a way, they had both lost their mothers as children: Da Ponte's mother had died when he was a child and Casanova felt abandoned by his actress mother who devoted more attention to the stage than to her son, and perhaps part of their obsession with women was a restless search for the affection they felt had eluded them as children. They both had vestiges of a religious sensibility: Da Ponte had been ordained a priest, though effectively never practiced as one; Casanova went to the seminary, but decided the priesthood was not for him after finding himself happily seduced by a woman.

The lascivious Casanova regarded himself as a kind of mentor to Da Ponte, and shared many of the experiences that were later recorded in his well-written but indelicate 12-volume *History of My Life*, which he began in 1786 when he moved to the ornate surroundings of Count Walstein's castle in Bohemia, where he was to manage the aristocrat's extensive library. In this excessively long account of why his existence mattered so much to the world, Casanova not only relived his experiences; he also reinvented them. Although the external history is accurate, the master seducer used his fertile imagination to enhance and exaggerate the details of his private life. Casanova's extravagant imagination gave Da Ponte fertile ideas for the plot of *Don Giovanni*.

Da Ponte was a highly intelligent man but not an original mind. As a child he had displayed a stupendous ability to memorize entire chunks of ancient Greek and Latin literature, and could recite Dante's *Inferno* by heart. So in writing the libretto to *Don Giovanni*, he synthesized elements from Casanova's imagination with earlier versions of the Don Juan myth. However, Da Ponte did not borrow from Casanova's own character. Unlike Casanova, who was consumed with the desire to please the women he hunted, the figure of Don Giovanni that Da Ponte created seeks only to master and conquer women, showing no compunction about destroying them utterly in the process. Despite the titillating ingredients and the superlative music of Mozart the opera is haunted by this dark force. One wonders what Casanova made of it: since he was living nearby, Casanova was able to attend the first performance of *Don Giovanni* on October 29, 1787, in Prague, the capital of Bohemia.

Writing operas about Don Giovanni was certainly a fashionable choice in eighteenth-century Europe. Mozart's was the fourth opera on this libertine in 1787 alone. By the time his version first premiered in Prague in October of that year, three other operas on the subject had already appeared that same year in Italy, two in Venice and one in Rome. However, Mozart's version was more than a cut above the rest: it was in a different league altogether. Despite the flaws in Da Ponte's cheeky libretto, especially apparent in the closing scene, what really elevated Mozart's *Don Giovanni* above rival versions was the exquisite way in which Mozart's genius made up for the shortcomings in the script with sublime music that provided a perfect foil for this compelling tale of a serial seducer.

Mozart's *Don Giovanni* opens with the tumultuous sound of the whole orchestra playing the D minor chord. Minor chords generally tap into a sense of sadness, if not tragedy. This D minor chord is no exception. Indeed the sense of anxiety is intensified by the fact that it is not simply one section of instruments playing, but the orchestra in its entirety. It is as though every musical instrument is in agreement. They all anticipate the events to come with foreboding and issue a dire warning. Each of the two opening chords is followed by a brief but deathly silence. The strings come in with a ghostly sound, again suggesting death and judgment. They play softly, as though hesitant, almost afraid of what is to happen, but the volume rapidly increases. Soon Mozart introduces four successive harmonic minor scales that sound like the sinister whoosh of a ghost rising up out of a grave. They produce an uncanny and eerie sound. The notes in each scale climb upwards like steps of a ladder, increasing in volume, before falling back down the steps of the ladder, as the volume diminishes. And each scale starts on a higher note than the one before, heightening the spectral quality. This initial part of the overture seems to be telling us that Don Giovanni is thoroughly sinister, and deserves to be judged severely.

But the overture abruptly changes character, moving from D minor into the corresponding major scale of D. Suddenly everything is joyful, light, buoyant, full of impetuosity and hope. Mozart is presenting the other half of Don Giovanni: his spontaneity, charm, and vivacity, his ceaseless chase after pleasure. This second part of the overture brims over with life and promise. There is the occasional anxious undercurrent, but any suggestion of foreboding is quickly submerged in an immense tide of joy. This second part of the overture suggests the carefree abandon of an unthinking child.

As the singing of the opera begins, we hear Don Giovanni's servant Leporello complaining about his difficult conditions of employment. As usual he is forced to do the unappetizing job, keeping night watch for his master outside the Commendatore's house in Seville while Don Giovanni seduces the Commendatore's daughter inside. As Leporello continues to grumble, the masked Don Giovanni rushes out of the house, pursued by Donna Anna. It is fitting that Don Giovanni wears a mask since he continually deceives people and constantly hides his real intentions. He is careful to veil the vulgar nature of his desires as much as possible. He wants women to fall for the fantasies he fabricates. There is something demonic in his constant lies, manipulation and evasiveness. Yet for all his craftiness, his true face somehow shows through to Donna Anna. Her screams draw the attention of her father, who is then killed by a thrust of Don Giovanni's sword.

As for Don Giovanni, he cannot bear to stay around, for then he might have to face the unpleasant truth about himself. He promptly departs along with Leporello. Donna Anna's fiancé, Don Ottavio, arrives at her side. Don Ottavio will supposedly help Donna Anna in her quest to avenge the killing of her father. But he looks a most unpromising candidate. If Don Giovanni is not ideal marriageable material, neither is Don Ottavio ideal heroic material. Don Ottavio is not the man any woman would instinctively turn to when the chips are down. Presumably he finds himself at Donna Anna's side because there is simply no one else around. Don Ottavio is too diffident and deferential to find the strength to sacrifice himself for a higher goal, and his priggishness would make it impossible for him to seize leadership and embrace the risks necessary to respond adequately to this demanding situation. Don Ottavio only manages to make an unconvincing vow to help her exact vengeance upon the assassin.

It is surprising that Mozart does not take advantage of Don Giovanni's murderous deed to elicit sympathy for Don Ottavio. After all, Don Ottavio would normally be expected to fill the role of hero. Instead Mozart chooses Don Giovanni as the star of the opera. In Mozart's time it was usual to cast the protagonist of the action in a favorable light: either as a valiant man from the beginning or as someone who attained heroic status as the plot unfolded. Therefore Don Ottavio would have been the likely candidate for the lead role in the opera. But in a revolutionary break with tradition, the "hero" of *Don Giovanni* is the villain, and Don Ottavio is the schoolboy prig. However, Don Giovanni's heroism is both limited in extent and unexpected in nature. He is a man who is only "heroic" in his final and stubborn refusal to repent, preferring the eternity of damnation to the moment's effort to express his sorrow and contrition. Is Don Giovanni afraid to countenance his own vulnerability? Is he even aware of it? Does his aristocratic lineage accord him such a privileged status that he is simply immune to any sense of responsibility? Is he an atheistic hero, totally breaking with religion and repudiating its moral standards of right and wrong? Does he lack an eternal perspective, is he bereft of faith in an afterlife, so that the threat of damnation carries no menace for him? Is he a human being at all or is he simply too shallow to be real, perhaps representing an elemental force of nature? The final possibility seems plausible, because Don Giovanni is bereft of self-knowledge from the start and does not learn anything about himself in the course of the opera. But then again, if as his servant Leporello claims, the Don has seduced over 2,000 women, surely he has had innumerable opportunities to reflect? Isn't it just conceivable that he might have reflected at least once?

But on the evidence of the opera, Don Giovanni never stops to reflect. His cowardly murder of the old man does nothing to halt his seductive spree. It does not even give him pause for reflection. Immediately after fleeing the scene of the crime he is back to his old ways — while talking animatedly to Leporello he suddenly catches the scent of a woman. The woman in question is Donna Elvira, whom he seduced in Burgos before unceremoniously dumping her. Donna Elvira's face is covered by a veil and at first the Don does not recognize her. He ostensibly approaches this damsel in distress to comfort her but in reality in order to add her to his list of conquests. Meanwhile she is pouring her pent-up rage and resentment at the man who abandoned her (who is in fact Don Giovanni) into a passionate aria, *"Ah chi mi dice mai,"* the beauty of which suggests that her love for the philanderer still lingers. Don Giovanni approaches and greets her with the sweetly sung word "Signorina." Elvira asks who is there. She drops the veil from her face and Don Giovanni discovers to his dismay that it is none other than Donna Elvira. As soon as she recognizes Giovanni, Elvira recounts the story of her sorry seduction at his hands and vents the anger that still grips her. He flees, running away not only from Donna Elvira but also from himself, and urges Leporello to engage her attention by reciting his master's interminable catalog of conquests. There follows the only aria to offer a panoramic survey of Don Giovanni's life, one that is not at all as revealing as it appears to be.

It is surprising that this aria is not sung by Don Giovanni; and even more astonishing that he never once sings a major aria himself. Just as the principal characters in a Shakespearean play have the opportunity to present themselves through a soliloquy, so the chief character in an opera traditionally has a significant aria in which to present the inner workings of his or her psyche. But in the case of Don Giovanni, we never get to see the inner man, so much so that we begin to wonder is there anything inside at all. Perhaps he is a force of nature rather than a credible creature of flesh and blood.

Ironically, although Don Giovanni himself is not on stage, it is at this point that we learn most about his character and conquests. It is through his sidekick Leporello that we get to know Don Giovanni better. Only Leporello and Donna Elvira are present. To the consternation of Donna Elvira, Leporello produces the meticulous record he has kept of all of the women seduced by his master, a record whose length exceeds Donna Elvira's worst fears. Leporello takes great satisfaction in keeping this prurient record up to date. It is as though he is the memory of Don Giovanni; indeed he becomes so absorbed in this account, that it is almost as if Don Giovanni himself were rendered on stage. Added to this is the fact that Leporello sings the aria in Don Giovanni's key of D major. In a sense, Leporello is the Don's inadequate and erratic conscience. Perhaps this explains why the character of Don Giovanni on his own is so humanly insubstantial — Leporello in fact may be the missing half of Don Giovanni.

In Joseph Losey's visually stunning film version of the opera, Leporello's book is like a thick concertina or accordion which he dramatically unfolds, layer after layer, upon the endless steps that descend from Don Giovanni's palatial residence. This is the celebrated and comic "Catalog Aria." Apparently the Don has seduced 91 women in Turkey, 100 in France, 231 in Germany, and 640 in Italy. But his greatest success has been in his native land of Spain, where 1,003 women have fallen under his sensual spell. The unusually high Spanish number becomes the refrain of this delightful aria: "ma in Ispagna son già mille e tre."

The grand total comes to 2,065. This vast number embraces women of every age, social status and physique. Don Giovanni is thoroughly democratic and ecumenical in his tastes. He has an appetite for country girls, city girls, waitresses, countesses, baronesses, marchionesses, princesses, blondes, brunettes, plump women, thin women, but above all the young beginner ("la giovin principiante"). As Leporello describes the innumerable kinds of women his master delights in, he sings up and down the scale as though catching every note just as the Don grabs every woman. Donna Elvira knew that Don Giovanni was a cad, but even she is shell-shocked by the sheer scale of his exploits.

Like Donna Elvira, most opera-goers take Leporello's word that the Don has seduced 2,065 women, and gasp in awe and indignation. But those spectators or listeners who pay close attention will make a curious discovery: despite the immense claims made on behalf of Don Giovanni by his servant Leporello, there is not a single woman who yields to Don Giovanni in the course of the entire opera. And the only woman who has willingly surrendered to him is Donna Elvira, and even that happened before the period of time covered by the opera. Thus we have male bravado taken to a ridiculous level of falsehood: Leporello boasts of the endless conquests of someone who in reality completely fails to conquer a single woman. The only woman with whom Don Giovanni has had his way is Donna Anna, and that is because he has violated her. In fact, if anything, Don Giovanni is more the pursued than the pursuer, and the women who are chasing him, Donna Elvira and Donna Anna, have no intention of seducing him: it is revenge they want. However, it is easy to fall for the misleading publicity campaign orchestrated by Don Giovanni's irrepressible servant Leporello. One is almost led to believe that the compulsively lustful Don Giovanni really is a roaring success. In reality the grand libertine is nothing of the sort. He may be pathologically fixated on women, but he completely fails to win them over. This failure is symptomatic of lust, which promises perfect satisfaction but only fills its victims with a gnawing hunger that rages inside. Unfortunately at times the more ridiculous the lies we are fed, the more likely we are to believe them.

Rather than describe the remainder of the opera in detail, let me simply select two more significant scenes. In the scene that follows the Catalog Aria, two young country people, Massetto and Zerlina, are about to celebrate their wedding. Don Giovanni and Leporello come upon the party and the Don instructs Leporello to ply Masetto and the other guests with food and wine while he "takes care" of the bride-to-be Zerlina. In an attempt to seduce her, Don Giovanni praises Zerlina's physical features and tells her that such beauty is living proof that she is destined for something much higher in life. He announces that he wants to marry Zerlina there and then. As he continues to woo her, the Don launches into the beautiful duet: "Là ci darem la mano." Don Giovanni invites Zerlina to take his hand and to become his. She is torn: she would like to succumb and yet she is unsure: "Vorrei e non vorrei." Aware of the gulf in class between them, she is also unsure of Don Giovanni's intentions. Moreover she cannot help thinking of Masetto, though Don Giovanni's persuasiveness soon induces forgetfulness of her groom. At the beginning of the duet Don Giovanni and Zerlina sing separately, but when she finally yields they sing in perfect synchronicity and absolute harmony: "let us go, let us go my dear one and ease the ache of an innocent love." The fervor of Don Giovanni suggests he may have come to believe in his own lie; in any case Zerlina certainly does. The magical duet works its effect and Don Giovanni and Zerlina skip off the stage arm in arm to a dancing rhythm. Luckily for Zerlina, Donna Elvira arrives just before Don Giovanni can fulfill his devious designs upon the innocent girl.

Because Don Giovanni sings such bewitching songs, it is easy to forget that in trying to seduce Zerlina on her wedding day, he is also effectively attempting to topple her impending marriage. The fact that Zerlina is a prospective bride adds to the challenge for Don Giovanni. The Don is all sweetness and charm but his agenda is devastatingly destructive. Lust has always been extraordinarily enticing because it is the capital sin which beckons with the greatest pleasure, but it is still deadly. As the life of Don Giovanni illustrates, the enormous thrill that lust offers is illusory and deceptive. The pleasure of lust lasts a moment, whereas the pain of succumbing to her aristocratic seducer would have haunted Zerlina's existence for a lifetime, destroying her relationship with Massetto.

Let's fast-forward to the closing scenes of the opera. Despite the efforts of Donna Elvira, Donna Anna and Ottavio to catch him, Don Giovanni is still at large. He is laughing with Leporello about his latest escapades when they both hear the ghostly voice of the Commendatore from the darkness of the graveyard where they find themselves. Apparently the statue at the Commendatore's grave has come to life. Leporello is terrified, but Don Giovanni is perfectly unruffled. He brazenly orders Leporello to invite the statue to dinner with them. When the statue arrives, there is an almighty clash of instruments before the statue sings the following words in a forbiddingly deep bass voice, practically all on the same note: 'Don Giovanni, you have invited me to dinner and I have come' ("Don Giovanni, a cenar teco m'invitasti e son venuto"). The statue repeatedly orders Don Giovanni to repent but the Don steadfastly refuses, despite his hand being held in an icy grip by this figure from beyond the grave. Having failed to repent of his sins, the Don cannot escape his terrible fate and is dragged down to the fiery flames of hell.

This final twist of the plot simply does not fit in with what has gone before, and confirms, if confirmation were needed, that the greatness of this opera lies in the music and not in the story. First of all, the punishment that is imposed on Don Giovanni is external. It would be much more credible were the punishment to unfold inevitably from within himself, from a sense of isolation, guilt, and some grudging admission of the havoc he causes to others. If you compare Mozart's *Don Giovanni* with Tolstoy's *Anna Karenina*, another great work of art, this becomes evident. In this outstanding Russian novel, the beautiful and vivacious Anna is plagued by guilt as a result of her affair with Vronsky; she feels bereaved when she has to give up her son, she is ostracized by polite society, and she becomes increasingly consumed by jealousy and spite. And the fact that she finally throws herself under a train, although deeply tragic, also has a tragic inevitability about it. But Don Giovanni's demise requires the intervention of someone else, and seems tagged on as a moral lesson. In the original Spanish Don Juan story, the protagonist was immeasurably more credible: he experienced fear because of his belief in the supernatural, and he sought to repent, but discovered to his grief that his time had run out. In *Don Giovanni*, the absurdly stupid Don is unbelievably complacent: although facing damnation, he cannot see any cause for concern. Da Ponte, in a last minute dash to get his libretto together, was probably unthinkingly copying from one of the many inferior Italian versions of the story that failed to convey the subtlety of the Spanish original. As for Mozart, although musically enthralled by his protagonist earlier in the opera, he ultimately returns to the first part of the opera's opening overture, unveiling the Don's sinister and dark side.

Don Giovanni's refusal to repent does not ring true to his character. After all, Don Giovanni has spent the whole opera fleeing responsibility, evading the consequences of his actions in a cowardly way, selfishly intent on self-preservation at all costs. But his sudden refusal to mend his ways is certainly not going to guarantee his continued survival; in fact, it promises to hasten his demise. Since he has displayed an unerring ability to save his own skin, why should he categorically refuse to do so when the punishment that faces him is more serious than ever before? Furthermore, even if he does not feel sorry, he is presumably the sort of character who would have no qualms about feigning repentance. It did not cost him a moment's hesitation to lie when falsehood served to further his amorous adventures. He told Zerlina preposterous lies, pledging to marry her immediately. The unexpected appearance of steely resolve in the previously flimsy character of Don Giovanni almost seems like courage.

In truth, there is nothing courageous about Don Giovanni's nonchalant stance. Almost two and a half thousand years ago, in his *Nichomachean Ethics,* Aristotle showed that brave people feel fear, especially when the occasion warrants it. And in Don Giovanni's case, the prospect of hell should elicit terror. Being courageous does not free us from fear. In fact it is a mistake to suppose that courage implies the absence of fear. On the contrary, courage and fear can coexist, especially when it comes to taking noble actions. For noble deeds demand personal sacrifice and risk, and the emotion of fear alerts us to the high cost such actions may exact. Fear is a sign of mental health, and is thus worth listening to. There is something mad or insensible about persons without fear. It is worth paying attention to our fears, but making them the basis for our decisions is not advisable. This is where courage comes in. Courage gives us the strength to manage and master our fears, to act having listened to them, rather than acting out of them.

Don Giovanni appears brave because he is unafraid. However, he ought to feel afraid because the occasion warrants it. If he does not feel fear, there can be nothing heroic about his stubbornness, because there is nothing heroic about acting in ignorance. Don Giovanni appears brave because he is blithely unaware of the danger of damnation that he faces. But apart from the issue of fear, it is erroneous to talk of someone being courageous in pursuing evil. A person can only be courageous if the goal in question is a noble one. A courageous person knows what is truly worth giving up life and limb for. And since Don Giovanni has no noble end in mind, he does not deserve to be called courageous. In fact, Don Giovanni comes across as such a morally immature person as to be ignorant of the difference between right and wrong. Perhaps he should be given a course in moral education and development rather than sentenced to definitive annihilation.

The myth of Don Juan offers a certain interpretation of the mystery of human beings and the human world, and a deeply ambiguous one at that. For although it pretends to condemn Don Juan, the legend also secretly praises him. As the Nobel prizewinning Irish playwright George Bernard Shaw (1856-1950) pointed out in the play *Man and Superman* (which includes a long third act on Don Juan in Hell), the lesson that moralists attempt to impart is not always the one that hearers choose to listen to. Music or literature intended to warn people away from forbidden fruit often makes them more curious to eat it. The Don Juan myth is all the more powerful because it has entered into the collective unconscious of our culture. The James Bond series of films is a hugely popular contemporary variation of the myth: 007 seduces one girl after another, extricates himself from the most hopeless predicaments, saves civilization, and finds his worst behavior condoned with a knowing smirk by the end of each movie.

A lot of men would like to be as successful with the fairer sex as Don Giovanni claims to be, if only they could do it without destroying women in the process. And some women presumably find seduction at the hands of sexual supermen to be an absolutely tantalizing prospect. Perhaps they hope that they could be finally the one to tame him. Unfortunately, too many women end up going through a lot of useless suffering because they subscribe to the myth that they can "fix" bad men.

The irony is that although we can fool ourselves into believing that Don Giovanni is the greatest adventurer of them all, he is on the contrary a profoundly unadventurous man. He is addicted to the fix of continual conquests. He is so compulsive that his behavior is thoroughly predictable. In this sense the myth of Don Giovanni is a lie about love. This philanderer has reduced the range and intensity of his desires to a single and debilitating one: the desire to dominate and dump women, to consume them quickly and toss them immediately aside. The tragedy of Don Giovanni is that he is a man of such limited desire. He has hardly risked anything. Instead of really desiring life, he has indulged in a continual merry-go-round which has led him nowhere. Lust has destroyed him, whereas love would have created him.

Purity is the passion for someone greater than anything we could ever imagine — it is the singleness of heart that wholly desires God. It means living the wholeness of holiness not only in our souls but also in our bodies, not only in our desires but also in our deeds. And God, who is exceedingly generous, does not gauge our purity of heart with an infinite measure, because if that were the case, nobody's pure love, however immense, would amount to much. But God rates our generosity according to the capacities of our own hearts — if we give with all our hearts, that's what counts, no matter how small a particular heart may be. And luckily God does not reward in a human way by giving us the same measure back, or even a little more. As is evident from the miracles of the loaves and fishes in the Gospels, God does not add but multiplies. God gives an immense reward. As for lust, it is not only present in persons who commit the act but also in persons who actively desire to do so. Persons who trawl the web or watch films in order to arouse sensual feelings are at least as guilty as those who commit material acts of lust. Persons are contaminated by what comes from the eyes of their mind and the eyes of their bodies. Contaminated thoughts contaminate the body and soul. But the physical eyes also corrupt because an illicit affair generally starts with a lustful look.

It is worth reflecting on the stories of the Don Juan sort in order to be clear why it is not in our best interests to imitate their protagonists. Otherwise we might mistakenly believe we ought to revise our own lives to harmonize with their plots. But as Thomas Aquinas realized, the reason people sink into lower pleasures is because they have not sought higher ones. That is why G.K. Chesterton could make the audacious claim that the man knocking on a prostitute's door is really looking for God. Human beings are made for joy, and when they do not look for joy of a human and spiritual kind, they end up grabbing a most inadequate substitute. The truth which lustful people are often half-blind to is that they are not after sex, but something that their minds tell them will come with it — happiness, intimacy, union and love. Yet these things only accompany sex in a committed and reverential relationship of love, where the good of the other is actively sought.

Had Don Giovanni possessed the capacity for self-reflection, he would have begun to see through his veneer of self-serving satisfaction. It is precisely the purity of perfect love that he is seeking in all the wrong ways: unknown to himself, in wanting every woman, he wants something much more than any one woman can give, for he wants God. The Don is restlessly searching for something that is painfully lacking in his life: a sense of unconditional acceptance and perfect belonging. But he hides the pain from himself by embarking frenetically on a succession of momentary conquests. The incessant chase becomes the numbing anesthetic. And the fact that he abandons each woman as soon as she surrenders is a sign that the great love he incessantly dreams of finding turns out to be an empty illusion every time, and never a resolution.

The Don does not love because he never seeks the well-being of any of these women, although he wants everything from them. It is all one-way traffic for he insists on doing it *his* way. He will go to any lengths to deceive women, in order to get what they are unable to give him — total acceptance and complete satisfaction. He wants to be wanted and instinctively senses that he won't be wanted for long by any one woman. He knows that they will see through his empty charade sooner rather than later. So he leaps from one affair to the next to make himself believe that he is loved. But brief bodily togetherness cannot satisfy the perfect personal connection he is after.

Don Giovanni is engaged in a fruitless exercise: he uses a band-aid to cover a gaping wound, for he attempts to heal his spiritual emptiness by means of physical fullness. But despite knowing deep down that he is not finding true joy, he at least feels he will get guaranteed pleasure in sex, however brief it lasts. But the fleeting moment of pleasure is all he ever gets, over and over again. The everlasting monotony of spiritless and marked-down sex destroys him. The heavenly music that accompanies his sorry quest almost beautifies the ugly evidence, were it not for the brutal realities of a murdered man and a host of deceived women. It is not just harmless fun. It is life-destroying.

How could Don Giovanni break the cycle? With difficulty. He would need outstanding motivation and discipline, allied to the gift of God's grace; he would also need a new vision of life. He would need to see truths much more wonderful than the falsehoods that have undermined him, truths that Christianity dares him to believe. First of all he must realize that there are more things in human love than he has ever dreamed of. He needs to see that he is created for a sexual union extending far beyond the moment, so revolutionary as to make him one body with the woman he loves, and to interweave their identities to such an extraordinary degree that he can resonate with the passionate cry of Catherine in *Wuthering Heights*: "I am Heathcliff," as he sees in the woman a fellow human being whose startling capacity to love echoes the infinite love of God. And secondly he needs to discover the amazingly subversive reality of divine love. He needs to experience the stupendous fact that he is loved unconditionally by God, with a love that exceeds in depth and intensity any joy he has ever experienced; and perhaps it might also dawn on him that this love was sealed by the blood of Jesus who would have gladly died on the cross for him alone, were he the only sinner in need of salvation. If Don Giovanni could wake up to this real vision, he could cast the nightmare of lust aside. This marvelous vision comes alive through self-giving.

If all the would-be Don Juans of this world could learn to see in this new way, they might stop feeding on paltry fragments and feast on inexhaustible food instead. They might stop limiting their lives with lust and begin to open themselves to the infinite mystery of love, which always beckons them beyond anything they could possibly desire or imagine. They might smash the petty idols they have made for themselves, and worship the true God who has fashioned them for so much more.

How can we arrive at a new vision of God, the world, and ourselves? The next two chapters give concrete steps and practical advice.

7

Living in the Light

*Even the darkness will not be dark to you; the night
will shine like the day.*

Psalm 139

*. . . If I stoop
Into a dark tremendous sea of cloud,
It is but for a time. I press God's lamp
Close to my breast; its splendour soon or late,
Will pierce the gloom. I shall emerge one day.*

Robert Browning (1812-1889)

Today we have many stupendous and time-saving ways
of communicating. But have you ever wondered how heavenly beings communicate? The apostle and evangelist John
is fond of saying that God is light and perhaps there is a clue
in that. I remember coming across the writings of one mystic who claimed that heavenly messages are transmitted by
a process of illumination: God illuminates the angels closest to him, and they in their turn enlighten the angels who
are on a lower level with this divine light.

Be that as it may, one of the most helpful pieces of advice I ever received in time of difficulty was connected with the theme of light. I was a young seminarian beset by questions, wondering whether I had made the right choice in life. I knew other young men of my age who seemed to be constantly drinking and partying, or so I thought. They were "scoring" regularly with girls, or so they claimed. Meanwhile I was living a lonely life amidst an elderly community of priests and getting zero affirmation from the unruly teenagers I tried to teach each day. I found myself constantly comparing my real situation with my unreal picture of the life everyone else was leading. It was like they were all inside a chocolate shop gorging while I shivered on the rainy windswept pavement outside, feeling totally excluded. At least that is how it seemed to me. I felt I was missing out on a lot of pleasure and, ashamed as I would have been to say it to anyone, I wanted some of the action. I longed to sink into the arms of a woman and forget my worries in her gentle caresses. A woman could teach me what life was about. Lustful desires began to whisper and ferment within me and they would not be silenced by any of the weak-willed resolutions I threw in their direction. I felt I was in a losing battle. Maybe it had even come to this — saying farewell to the path to priesthood.

Through God's providence, as I was chatting to a man of God about something else, he recalled a comment his professor once made at medical school: "Any surface exposed to the light loses its germs." Afterwards I figured that this man had read the struggle going on inside me by the pained look in my eyes. The phrase he uttered may sound like a self-evident truth, but it spoke to my heart in a deep way. I saw that the essential thing for me was to be transparent: to bring my inner temptations, anxieties, and doubts into the open, to be accountable to someone. Only then could I hope for healing.

I found a wise Jesuit, a true soul-friend, with whom I was able to bring my temptations and fears about impurity into the light, and both of us could then behold these temptations from the distance of wisdom. Once they were under the light, they no longer had the same hold over me. Now they were known by two, as well as being placed in the presence of a mysterious third, God himself, whose presence I always sensed in these sacred moments of soul-sharing. It was above all God who burned up the darkness within me, incinerating the black coals, turning them into ashes, and truly "enlightening" me. Only later did I discover that Ignatius of Loyola had recommended this very procedure in order to cope with the wiles of the devil. Ignatius knew secrecy to be one of the most powerful weapons of Satan, who hates being uncovered. In his *Spiritual Exercises*, Ignatius describes the devil as a false lover who encourages you to keep hidden everything going on inside. This is a strategy for keeping you imprisoned because this fallen angel knows that once you reveal your temptations and fears to a spiritual director, their grip upon you will loosen and they will most likely disappear.

Before he turned toward the light, Ignatius of Loyola was drawn by sparkle of a different kind — the conquest of romance, the intoxication of personal glory, and the dream of power. It was partly this ego-driven ambition that led him, on May 21st 1521, to risk death in a battle that had little importance in the wider scheme of things. Against all sound military advice, Ignatius persuaded 1,000 Spanish soldiers to stand by him in defending the walled Spanish city of Pamplona against a French army that was 13,000 strong. The French bombarded the Spanish defenders for six hours. Despite the stubborn courage of Ignatius and his willingness to fight against all odds, there was to be no miraculous victory for the Spanish. Instead they surrendered once Ignatius was hit by a cannonball that shattered his right knee. After a couple of weeks of treatment in Pamplona, Ignatius was carried back to his family house.

By this time Ignatius was so near death that the doctors gave up hope. He received the last rites on the eve of the feast day of Saints Peter and Paul. But within a few days a painfully slow yet surprisingly promising recovery began. Apart from the pain of having his leg repeatedly operated on to straighten it, the biggest challenge was the sheer monotony of life as a patient: he had to lie in bed for nine months before he was able to walk again.

Living in an age without the comforting distractions of television, radio, DVDs, and video games, Ignatius was predictably bored out of his mind as he lay on his bed. He asked for some reading material. Tales of romance and valor were what interested him, but as it happened the only reading material lying around the house was of a more spiritual nature, accounts of the life of Jesus and the saints. These were not the kinds of books he wanted, but since there was nothing else to do, Ignatius took them up and started to read.

A curious thing happened. This intensely ambitious and competitive man began to notice new desires at work inside him. Reading the stories of Jesus and the saints, and seeing their deeds of love with his mind's eye, Ignatius felt attracted by their way of life. Not that his former ambitions had died: he constantly and fondly pictured life as a chivalrous courtier and lady's man. So there was a new struggle as saintly and secular ambitions competed for his attention. Had he not been jolted into awareness by his cannonball experience and reduced to immobility by his wounds, Ignatius would not have got around to entertaining desires of the saintly kind. Because Ignatius had imagined himself to be happy in his previously egotistical existence, he had absolutely no reason to consider changing it.

If we are pursuing our own pleasure in a self-seeking way of life, we are unable to hear God's voice unless we get a wake-up call. And that is one of the reasons that God uses not only literal cannonball experiences, but also figurative ones, to rouse us from our moral stupor. However, it is not as though God sets out to punish us: God is not vengeful. In fact, God's approach is full of respect for our freedom: "I stand at the door and knock" (Revelation 3:20). A helpful analogy to understand what is at issue is this: imagine a householder who enjoys hosting friends of dubious morality. Suppose one day a truly good person knocks at his door. The man will in all likelihood feel uncomfortable and ill-at-ease, not because the virtuous person is out to take over his house or attack him, but precisely because the bearing and words of this good human being arouse a sense of guilt in the morally bad man. The good person is perhaps only trying to get through to this man, yet this act of compassion is unwelcome because he experiences it as a judgment on his own misdeeds. He will be tempted to slam the door shut. A man leading a morally bad way of life may first experience God's call as guilt-inducing or as showing up the futility of his own life by comparison.

However, it is important to stress that anyone who experiences sadness and despair does not pick up these inner movements from God. This is not to deny that people feel sadness and despair, but simply to make clear that the origin of these overwhelming and negative emotional moods is not divine. Certainly a person who leads a bad life may experience the sting or pain of remorse at the approach of God. Sorrow and repentance can take the form of a strong disgust for sin, joined to the desire not to sin again. But sadness and despair neither come from God nor lead toward him. Sadness almost always comes from an evil spirit, and tends to diminish our appetite and energy for doing what is good. It makes us lose heart in the face of even small difficulties so that we quickly become dejected. Despair is always from the evil one. Despair means that a person freely and fully loses all hope of being saved and inheriting eternal life. It is the erroneous belief that salvation is impossible, either because our sins are so terrible that we are convinced God could not possibly forgive us, or because we doubt God's willingness to forgive us in any case. Despair effectively denies the goodness and mercy of God. Despair wreaks utter havoc when people bereft of hope abandon themselves completely to evil.

Ignatius no doubt felt the contradictory pulls of sorrow versus sadness, of repentance versus despair, during the long summer of 1521. One biblical way of viewing the discernment that began to take shape in Ignatius' life at that time is through the illumination offered by the Gospel of Saint John, which speaks of light as life, and darkness as death. In the prologue to his Gospel, John describes Jesus as the light of humanity, a light that shone in the darkness but which the darkness did not comprehend (John 1:4-5). The verb that John uses in the original Greek of the Gospel is so rich in meaning that it could signify much more than simply "comprehend" in English. It could also mean any of the following: to encompass, grasp, accept, welcome, receive, value, master, assimilate, overcome or control. In John's Gospel there is tension, indeed downright opposition, between the light and the darkness. The darkness wants to grasp, overcome and master the light, but it cannot. The light continues to shine. And this is also the case inside our hearts: despite the fact that we are fallen and fragile creatures, rays of light still shine within us. The darkness is never absolute, although at times it seems to eclipse the sun. Saint Ignatius struggled with the shadows and strained towards the light.

So how come Ignatius became willing to listen to God's voice during his convalescence? What opened his eyes to the light? Obviously the fact of being injured did not of itself turn Ignatius from immaturity and selfishness to authenticity and love. But it did mark the beginning of a spiritual journey: it encouraged him to reflect about his life, and once he was carried back to Loyola, his reflection quickened and intensified. He received the sobering news that he was unlikely to recover and that his life was at an end. He was advised that all he could do was prepare for death; and it is a well known fact that there is nothing quite like death to focus the mind. Ignatius repented of his sins and received the last rites of the Church.

Ignatius did not die. Instead God set about raising him up spiritually. Because the sober surroundings of his family house offered Ignatius little opportunity to distract himself from his interior world, he had the time and energy to think through what these different life scenarios were saying to him. Because of the spiritual search that accompanied his close brush with death, Ignatius was now more than willing to entertain thoughts of a spiritual nature. In retrospect it was a blessing that his recovery was gradual. Had he been miraculously restored to full health, he would probably have returned immediately to his swashbuckling existence. He would never have had the leisure truly to see or the unhurried time to listen in a profound way.

Change became a real possibility for Ignatius as he lay on his sick bed, for he was visited by God, not in a direct vision of the sort Isaiah had in the Temple, but in an indirect yet real way through the temple of his imagination. The ground for this visitation had been prepared by his spiritual quest in the wake of his battle injury at Pamplona. Although God spoke to Ignatius through the world of imagination, this does not mean that the imagination is an infallible guide. It is more like an open field, subject to diverse and conflicting forces, and so can be influenced for evil as well for good. There is no getting away from the fact that the imagination is ambiguous. It is often rightly associated with fantasy, with escaping from reality, with illusions and delusions, and that was precisely how it worked when Ignatius pictured the noblewoman he would like to woo, or the warrior-like exploits he wanted to perform. These daydreams were a temptation to flee reality. Ignatius wanted to live in the magical and unreal world of fantastic exploits and never-ending romances. We can certainly conjure up magical pictures of ourselves with the imagination, but if these images draw us to a way of life that is only for self, they are unhelpful.

At the beginning Ignatius must have thought that the images of Jesus and the saints had little to do with his own concrete reality. Saintly virtue and spiritual heroism were infinitely beyond his powers. And yet one of the extraordinary gifts of the imagination is to enable us see similarity where others only see difference. The wonder of the graced imagination is that it can break into our "now," our present, and redeem us from the slavery of the past while opening us up to a liberating future. Indeed, certain thinkers have gone so far as to suggest that the imagination may be a secular name for the soul. It is more accurate to say that the imagination is a privileged way in which the soul sees. For the soul does not only "see" through the physical eyes and through the light of reason, but also by the stupendous ability of the imagination to make present realities that are physically absent.

During those long months of recuperation, Ignatius' imagination brought the world beyond the walls of his house to him. He was physically unable to stir from his bed, yet his soul was powerful enough to take the outer world into itself, not only through vivid memories from the past, but also through anticipation of a possible future world, of the person he could become, if only he wanted to.

As Ignatius pictured two different styles of life in his mind's eye, he noticed they caused two diverse reactions. He found that he was completely enthralled when he read novels about knights in shining armor or dreamed about making a career for himself. He really enjoyed these experiences while they lasted, but crucially only as long as they lasted. Once they were over and he had stopped focusing on them, he felt empty and desolate inside. But when he turned to biblical stories and legends about the saints and mulled over the possibility of becoming a disciple of Jesus, Ignatius found that he was not only filled with joy and consolation, but even after he had ceased thinking about them the sense of consolation remained.

Notice the priority of interiority — Ignatius gaze was turned inwards, examining his own heart. But even though Ignatius looked inside, he did not place his trust in his own willpower and motivation. Instead he listened to the flux of desires attracting him in different directions. His listening was accompanied by the dawning realization that one set of desires guided him towards God and goodness, while the other web of desires threatened to misguide and ensnare him. But for all this talk of interiority, externals are still important and should not be neglected. The reason Ignatius experienced these different wavelengths was because of the concrete experiences he had had up until then, because of what he had seen with his own eyes, as well as the books he had read, and the daydreams resulting from what he saw and read. The eye is the lamp of the body, and what the eye sees, whether really before it or by means of the imagination, affects the mind and heart. That is why Jesus advises his disciples to be vigilant when it comes to the eyes, because corrupt eyes will corrupt everything else.

Ignatius' discovery of the importance of interiority, of the heart, was nothing new. Jesus addressed this issue long before him. When the Pharisees accused his disciples of flouting the law by failing to wash their hands before eating, Jesus countered by insisting the cleanliness that really counts is cleanliness of the heart. Jesus showed that purity was an inner quality, since the desires and thoughts that issue from the heart are what make us clean or unclean. "But the things that come out of the mouth come from the heart, and these make a man 'unclean.' For out of the heart come evil thoughts, murder, adultery, sexual immortality, theft, false testimony, slander" (Matthew 15:18-19). It is precisely this sensitivity to the movements of the heart that Ignatius rediscovered.

Ignatius had dwelt upon images of personal glory and careerism on the one hand, and images of service of God and neighbor on the other. However, he did not immediately understand that one scenario was deathly and the other life-giving. He only arrived at this insight through a process of inner weighing and sifting. Obviously the best option of all would have been for Ignatius to open himself only to those desires that drew him toward God. However, at this initial stage of his spiritual journey, Ignatius did not possess the requisite maturity.

In the Gospels, the disciples also fail to see the danger of dreaming of personal glory. They ask Jesus to tell them who is the greatest in the kingdom of heaven, and are taken aback to discover that God's standard of greatness differs radically from human conceptions of power and status. Jesus calls a little child to him and explains that the greatest in heaven is someone who humbles himself like this child (Matthew 18:1-5). In another episode the disciples return from ministry overjoyed that demons have submitted to them. But Jesus insists that they should not be joyful on account of the power they experience over demons, but because their names are written in heaven (Luke 10:20).

The disciples' discernment, like that of Ignatius, matured over time. As part of Jesus' final teaching to the disciples before his death, he explained that the Spirit would lead and guide them into the truth (John 16:13). This is indeed what happened. Once the Spirit descended upon the apostles at Pentecost, they immediately developed the habit of making their decisions under the guidance of the Spirit. In Acts Chapter 15, regarded by many Scripture scholars as

Act's most decisive chapter, the apostles and elders assembled in Jerusalem made the irrevocable decision to open the Church to non-Jews. Commenting on how they arrived at their decision, they said that "It seemed good to the Holy Spirit and to us . . ." (Acts of the Apostles 15:28). The early Christians only recognized a decision as Christian if it was made under the inspiration of the Holy Spirit, for they sensed that the Holy Spirit was the soul of the Church, the one who kept it alive with his divine breath.

But what is discernment, and who is the Holy Spirit, and how does he help us grow into purity of love? It is time to answer these questions.

8

Guided by the Spirit

While Apollos was at Corinth, Paul took the road through the interior and arrived at Ephesus. There he found some disciples and asked them, 'Did you receive the Holy Spirit when you believed?' They answered, 'No, we have not even heard that there is a Holy Spirit.'

(Acts of the Apostles 19:2)

It is a beautiful and salutary thought that, wherever people are praying in the world, there the Holy Spirit is, the living breath of prayer. It is a beautiful and salutary thought to recognize that, if prayer is offered throughout the world, in the past, in the present and in the future, equally widespread is the presence and the action of the Holy Spirit, who "breathes" prayer in the heart of man in all the endless range of the most varied situations and conditions . . . Prayer is also the revelation of that abyss which is the heart of man: a depth which comes from God and which only God can fill, precisely with the Holy Spirit.

John Paul II, *Dominum e Vivificantem [Lord and Giver of Life]*

In 399 BC, as he faced the Athenian jury that would condemn him to death, the great philosopher and sage Socrates declared that the unexamined life was not worth living (see Plato, *Apology* 38a). These strong words were part of Socrates' last testament, and reflected his profound conviction that spiritual growth was impossible without the kind of examination that occurs through personal reflection and dialog with others. He had witnessed his contemporaries climbing the ladders of success, fame, wealth and pleasure without ever asking themselves if they were ascending the correct ladders. Because they had never paused to reflect, they had mistaken as truth the superficial answers provided by their culture. They had never asked their own questions, or if they did, they had not followed through and come up with their own answers; they had uncritically accepted the answers others gave them. Socrates preferred a life characterized by personal reflection. But though Socrates was passionately convinced of the value of an examined life, he did not believe that we should remain eternally immobile in reflection. He did not advocate the "paralysis of analysis" — reflection was at the service of the practical purpose of living better.

Self-examination is also an important element in the life of a Christian: "Examine yourselves to see whether you are in the faith; test yourselves" (2 Corinthians 13:5). And as in the case of Socrates, Christian discernment is at the service of life. It is for the sake of loving God and others better. It is not introspective navel-gazing but entails an encounter with the mysterious otherness of the Spirit. Christian discernment is a joint venture between God and the human being. With God's help, we can bring order to the innumerable impulses, moods, feelings and thoughts that swirl inside us, identifying and strengthening those that lead to God, and unmasking and rejecting those that turn us away from God. God is not an absentee landlord; he is not far away from us. In fact he is at work in our hearts, stirring our thoughts and affections, either directly as God the Holy Spirit or through an angelic messenger.

Discernment is not a matter of merely human powers of reflection. Discernment is only possible with the help of the Holy Spirit. Because of his very nature, the Spirit is more than willing to help. But like the disciples Paul met in Ephesus, some people have never even heard of the Holy Spirit. Many of those who have heard of the Holy Spirit don't know much more about him than the name. First of all, and most importantly, the Holy Spirit is God: along with the Father and the Son, he is one of the three persons of the Holy Trinity. The Holy Spirit is the personification of the ineffable love between the Father and the Son. The love between the Father and the Son is so unimaginably great that it makes a third Person, the Holy Spirit, who is equal to the Father and the Son. The Holy Spirit is pure love. The Holy Spirit is the innermost nature of God, a perfect love that continually shares itself. The Holy Spirit is the sheer ecstasy of God, his ever abundant and overflowing love. The Holy Spirit is the greatest gift God could give us, because the Holy Spirit is not just any kind of love, but God himself as love. The Holy Spirit is God as love and God as gift. Because he is God and Person, the Holy Spirit is the greatest personal gift we could ever receive.

There are many images of the Spirit in Scripture — for example breath, wind, water, tongues of fire, dove and seal. They evoke someone alive and creative, powerful and gentle, beautiful, pure and unfathomable. Scripture also tells us a sensational and surprising truth — the Spirit is within us (John 14:17). If we pay attention to our inner being, we will hear his voice like an invigorating *breath* that revives us or a *wind* that raises us up. Our inner selves thirst for the living *water* which can become a river of joy within us, sending streams of grace flowing from us. Through prayer we can feel the warmth of the gentle flames of his blazing *fire*. He is the pure white *dove* whose beauty awakens us to life and helps us to spread our wings and fly joyfully in the boundless heavens, far transcending the restricted confines of our faint-hearted beings. He is the *seal* who stamps us with the intoxicating fragrance of thousands of blooming flowers in a lush meadow, whose stamp removes the stain of sin, who seals us too against demons and strengthens us in the struggle against evil. Because the Holy Spirit is *Holy*, he is completely pure and undefiled, perfect love and goodness. Therefore he attracts us toward the unfathomable goodness of God, unleashing transformative possibilities in our lives. Because the Holy Spirit is *Spirit*, he is without a body, and although personal, he is not confined by space and time, but is continually present everywhere. Because he is Spirit, he gives us the purposeful creativity of his overflowing life, making us a new creation, more ourselves rather than less human. "If you knew the gift of God . . . you would have asked him and he would have given you living water" (John 4:10).

Ignatius, as we saw in the last chapter, began to see that the Holy Spirit was gently murmuring in his heart. Sometimes the Holy Spirit speaks directly within, sometimes through the ministration of an angel. Ignatius was also aware of the destructive influence of the evil spirit within. As we saw earlier, the evil spirit refers primarily to Satan and other demons, but can also refer to the latent evil in our own hearts, in other people or indeed the evil that is found in society; all these evil influences can affect our feelings, thoughts, words and deeds. The task of discernment is to distinguish the good impulses from the bad ones, in order to follow the prompting of the good interior movements. We all experience contrasting moods, desires, feelings and thoughts inside — some are noble and generous, others are selfish and even depraved. We instinctively know that some of the evil desires that rise in our hearts should absolutely not be acted upon. But there are other occasions when we are ignorant and confused, and we end up doing what caused Paul such regret: "I do not understand what I do. For what I want to do I do not do, but what I hate I do" (Romans 7:15).

Saint Paul had an unrivalled knowledge of the objective rules and norms of religion. Yet despite his intimate familiarity with the theory of good and evil, he found that putting the commandments into practice was something else altogether. Ignatius of Loyola was no different. Immediately after his conversion, Ignatius almost fell prey to violent and evil impulses within him. Riding his mule on the way to Barcelona, he met a Moor and fell into conversation with him. As soon as the subject turned to religious matters, a heated debate arose, with the Moor arguing that the Virgin Mary had not remained a virgin all her life while Ignatius insisted on her perpetual virginity. After they finished, Ignatius experienced pangs of guilt because he felt he had not defended the Blessed Virgin robustly enough. Not sure what course of action to take, Ignatius decided to relax the reins of his mule and if the mule decided to follow the road taken by the Moor, he would kill the Moor, whereas if the mule took the other path, Ignatius would let the Moor live. The mule, wiser than his master, did not follow the path of the Moor. This story goes to show that even someone who sincerely seeks to serve God is capable of making terrible mistakes. Ignatius should have been aware of the inviolable nature of the commandment not to kill: instead he veered close to the kind of religious fanaticism that perpetrates evil deeds while invoking the name of God. In theory, the commandment "Thou shalt not kill" should have been abundantly clear to Ignatius, and he should have been able to see that it was sacred too in these circumstances. But in practice, he became confused because of a mixture of guilt and anger.

A life lived in fidelity to the commandments does not exempt us from the need for discernment. As we follow the path of the commandments, situations that invite discernment inevitably arise. Some experiences call for major discernment. Consider the story of the rich young man who approaches Jesus in Chapter 19 of Matthew's Gospel. He asks Jesus what good he must do in order to attain eternal happiness. Jesus explains that he must keep the commandments if he wants to enter into life. The young man responds that he has kept all the commandments from his youth and asks what else he lacks. He evidently wants to do something more with his life. Jesus replies that if he wants to be perfect he must sell all he has, give the money to the poor and follow him. But when the young man hears these words, his face becomes downcast and he walks away sorrowfully because he is a man of great wealth.

The fact that the rich young man felt there was something lacking in his life indicates that he was in touch with his inner self. In order to be able to discern at all, we must be attuned to our inner feelings and moods. Inside us there is a continual stream of tendencies and drives pulling us in different directions. The young man was in contact with this inner world and this is why he sensed an indistinct drawing to something more, something he himself could not quite put his finger on. It was Jesus who identified this vague yearning for him: a desire for pure love, concretized in giving up everything in order to be solely and fully for Christ. The Holy Spirit was drawing the young man toward the fullness of life and toward the deeds necessary to arrive at this fullness. That is why he felt the desire and longing to be more generous in serving God.

The evil spirit knew that the young man's weak point was wealth — not just the money itself but the security net it guaranteed him. And this became the stumbling block for him, the obstacle that impeded his progress. The evil spirit introduced fear into his heart at the prospect of losing his possessions and his secure position in life. The young man paid more attention to the voice of the evil spirit than to the Holy Spirit's voice, and so he decided not to follow Jesus.

The Gospel notes that the young man went away sad. He was evidently already aware at that moment that he was missing out on joy and happiness by refusing the invitation of Jesus. He knew he had refused the opportunity to be more generous with his soul. When we are at peace with our conscience as that young man was because of living the commandments, we experience joy in the aftermath of following the call of God, and sadness when we turn away from it, just like Ignatius did on his convalescent bed. Although as a rule sadness does not come from God, it seems that the sadness or sense of disappointment felt by the young man at this moment may indeed have come from the Holy Spirit. After all, the evil spirit would never want to elicit sadness in the heart of someone who turned away from Jesus. Were the evil spirit to do that, he would be working against himself and effectively undermining his own efforts. It would seem to be the Holy Spirit who moved the young man's spirit to sadness. The Holy Spirit initially drew the young man toward fuller life and subsequently inspired a feeling of sadness when he decided to turn away from Jesus. The Holy Spirit was working on two fronts or in two different ways in this youth's heart — inviting him to realize his noble desires, and bringing about unease when he turned away from these higher goals.

We do not know what happened after the rich young man left the presence of Jesus. The end of the story was not the end of his story. Hopefully the sadness that enveloped him at that moment did not thicken and turn him away from goodness. I like to imagine that he recovered his serenity and continued to follow the precepts of life, even if he only gave of himself in a measured and imperfect way. Perhaps he always lived with the regret of knowing he could have dared so much more.

The rich young man was confronted with a major vocational decision. But for the most part, discernment is a valuable way of finding God's plan for us in the little experiences that make up everyday life. Suppose you are following God's commandments with purpose and consistency. One day you are waiting in line in a store and your attention is caught by the stream of MTV images on the television behind the counter. It is not a channel you would normally choose if you had a remote in your hand. But because of the direction of the queue, there is not much else to focus your eyes on at that moment, or so you persuade yourself. You thrill at the life and the carefree abandon of what you see, though you also feel a vague hint of unease at the sexy images of gyrating figures that flash across the screen. If you have developed the habit of discernment, you can take quick and effective action in a situation like this. If not, you may end up fooling yourself by saying something like "Continuing to watch this will really help me understand my college friends," or "Looking at the screen for a couple more minutes won't do me any harm." If you are practicing discernment, you will immediately put yourself in the presence of God and ask for his guidance. In God's presence you attune yourself to the feelings and impulses that are stirred by these images. "Do the emotions and thoughts generated by these images bring me closer to you, Lord? If I continue to watch this, will my relationship with you deepen? Will I be honoring you by fixing my eyes on these images?" You might be inspired by the Spirit to look instead at the people standing in line in front and behind you, and to carry them in prayer before Jesus so that he may touch them with the holiness of his divine heart.

Suppose you are a lay Christian minister, full of idealism and blessed with an affectionate spirit. Your parish sponsors you to do an intensive M.A. in Organizational Management, with the understanding that you will use this qualification to serve your parish and diocese. You are delighted. You talk with your experienced spiritual director, a woman who understands you well, and she agrees this is what God seems to be calling you to right now. You find the program academically rigorous, intellectually stimulating, and hard work. You learn a lot about how to manage both human and financial resources, and acquire skills in strategic planning, conflict management and other important areas. You have a strong feeling that this is what God wants you to be doing right now. Toward the end of each day, you allot 45 minutes to prayer in the beautiful oratory attached to your local parish church. You enjoy the change of rhythm and the opportunity to be in God's presence, sheltered at least temporarily from pressures and deadlines.

After a couple of weeks, you decide to lengthen your period of evening prayer, without informing your spiritual director. You find yourself drawn to pray about Christ's sufferings and the experience affects you so deeply that you are repeatedly moved to tears. In the days and weeks that follow you cry profusely, almost every evening. Your tutor notices that your grade average has dropped. He expresses surprise and disappointment at the level of your academic performance. He asks if you are going through an emotionally difficult period. You tell him that things could not be better, though inside you feel disappointed at your grades and wonder if this M.A. is simply too much for you. As you leave his office, you suddenly recall the deep emotions you are experiencing each evening as you contemplate the passion of Christ. You also realize that you have not spoken to your spiritual director about your lengthier prayer periods and the emotions that are surfacing. You think of phoning her but you tell yourself she is already too busy and in any case you are reluctant to bother her with your trivial concerns. Anyway, she might not really understand you. Besides, your spiritual life is full of consolation — you are praying well and being deeply touched by God.

Strange as it may seem, the strong affective dimension in your prayer may not be leading you to God at all. Certainly prayer itself is godly and I do not intend to say anything against it. Prayer is crucial, more vital for the life of the soul than oxygen is for the body. The problem is not the fact that you are praying, but that during these months of intensive study you unwisely resolved to prolong your period of daily prayer without mentioning it to your director, leading to increased tiredness and little motivation for the task at hand. You freely entered this intensive M.A., and after discernment with your spiritual director saw that God was calling you to this. But now because of your tears, you have lost your enthusiasm for the hard business of study, and you have major doubts about your ability to continue. Strong emotions are mentally draining, like a continual undercurrent that undermines your capacities, concentration and focus.

Your spiritual director, knowing that you have a strongly emotional character, would have advised you against lengthening your daily period of prayer. She would have suggested you temper your generosity. But Satan has taken advantage of your generosity. Because of your fundamental goodness, he knows that you would recognize and thwart a direct attack of his, so he chooses a more devious option, starting with an apparently loving thought that seems to be in harmony with your Christian commitment. However the results of this good inspiration show that it is not the work of the Holy Spirit, but of the evil spirit. The evil spirit knows that your emotionally volatile temperament is a potential point of weakness, and therefore an easier entry point for him. He knows where you are most vulnerable. The evil spirit suggests the initially good thought of prolonging prayer in order afterwards to destroy your peace and persuade you to give up your course of studies. Furthermore, the evil spirit is trying to convince you to keep your unease and discomfort hidden from your spiritual director through various specious lines of reasoning — her supposed heavy workload, the apparently insignificant nature of your problem, and your newfound suspicion that she does not understand you. As usual, Satan weaves a web of plausible lies. He knows that if you bring these subtle temptations into the light, you will see what is really going on with the help of your director, and his power will be broken.

Now that we have seen some concrete examples of discernment, it is worth asking how we can get in touch with these interior movements in our own lives. We can discover these movements best with the help of someone else to whom we are connected or accountable, a soul friend or spiritual director. But there are also some general guidelines to enable us decipher for ourselves how the Holy Spirit speaks to us and how the evil spirit does. Ignatius of Loyola developed these principles as a result of paying careful attention to his own conflicting moods and identifying where they were leading. Here are some of these guidelines.

How do the contrasting spirits work in egoistic people? Persons whose lives are already headed in a selfish direction make the evil spirit's work much easier. All he has to do is to confirm and comfort them in their choice. He does not need to act against them, because they are already on his side. It is enough for him to continue to feed their imaginations with images of sensual and selfish pleasures. These images will function as a pleasant anesthetic, so that they will feel smugly content at the prospect of committing more bad deeds. On the other hand, the Holy Spirit tries to get such persons to change the directions of their lives. He appeals to the goodness inside of them. Because the Holy Spirit wants them to make an about turn, his action will be experienced as discomforting, as a stinging of the conscience. He will induce a sense of remorse in order to rouse them from their selfish stupor.

How do the diverse spirits affect good people? In the case of persons who are actively leading good lives in God's service, the effects of the Holy Spirit and the evil spirit are practically the reverse of their effects in selfish people. In other words, the Holy Spirit confirms them in the path they have already taken, whereas the enemy tries to make them change direction. Satan is experienced in a negative way: he introduces sadness, puts obstacles in their path, and tries to undermine their peace with false reasons in order to retard their spiritual progress and reverse the direction of their lives. The Spirit of God, on the other hand, energizes and encourages them, inspiring them, bringing peace, consolation, removing obstacles and facilitating their path.

Once persons are on the path of spiritual growth, the Holy Spirit always has a positive effect upon them. In other words, the Divine Spirit prompts a positive affective mood in their hearts, called consolation. Consolation is a deep and lasting feeling of peace and joy that originates in God. Consolation is the personal experience of sensing a growth in faith, hope and love, which makes progress in goodness easier and more inviting.

Obviously, the evil spirit is not happy to see persons progress spiritually, and he tries to hinder them through enmeshing them in a negative web of feelings called desolation. Persons who are embarked on the journey towards goodness experience the evil spirit's action as desolating, as "de-souling" them, robbing them of their spiritual peace. Desolation attacks their faith, hope and love, and they find themselves losing interest in their relationship with God, doubting his love, drawn toward evil things, and so on. As a result it becomes more challenging to retain faith, hope and love.

It is vitally important that persons going through spiritual desolation stick with the good decisions they previously made. Being in desolation is a little like wearing sunglasses: everything around you looks much darker than it is, but in fact the problem is with you, not with the world. If you take off the sunglasses you will see things as they are. But if you make a decision based on your darkened perception of things, it could be disastrously wrong. Young and old, husbands and wives, priests and nuns, sometimes make this catastrophic mistake: they walk out of marriages, relationships, vocations, friendships and careers because they think the world is against them and others are at odds with them, when in fact it is they who are out of tune with themselves. It is their own gnawing restlessness that pushes them to fateful decisions, not other people or the rest of the world.

For instance, a seminarian who goes through a period of desolation, feeling separate from God and uninterested in prayer, distracted by women, and tempted to be unfaithful to his commitment, ends up thinking he should give up on his vocation. But if he is going to leave the seminary, he should not make such a decision while his perspective is distorted and blinded by inner frustration and dissatisfaction. It is like looking at stained-glass windows from outside a cathedral: they are always a disappointment. Later, when he recovers his serenity, he can by all means revisit the decision; he will then be able to make a good choice by acting out of a deep and embracing peace and contentment: now he will see life in its true splendor, like the viewer *inside* Chartres Cathedral who glories in the sunlight bursting through the hundred stained-glass windows of this magnificent medieval temple. No big decisions should be taken by persons who are spiritually down. Furthermore, rather than passively enduring desolation, they need to be proactive, and repel the desolation by taking decisive action and going on the counterattack, giving even more time than usual to prayer, self-examination, charity towards others and penance.

Ignatius also lists the three habitual ways in which the devil tries to undermine our Christian commitment, and shows the most effective ways of withstanding these attacks. First of all, Satan is like a chained dog — although this is not the particular image Ignatius uses, it conveys the substance of what he has to say. The "barking" of the evil one may be ferocious but it is essential to remember that he is tied up; only your fear can set him free. If you face him down and confront him, he will retreat like a coward. What Ignatius advises here is in effect a gloss on the Letter of Saint James which explains that if you stand firm against the devil he will run away from you (James 4: 7). But if you become discouraged and afraid, he will break loose from the chains and advance upon you, growing in power and ferocity. A quotation from Franklin D. Roosevelt's inaugural address of March 4, 1933 is especially apt here:

> So, first of all, let me assert my firm belief that the only thing we have to fear is fear itself — nameless, unreasoning, unjustified, terror which paralyzes needed efforts to convert retreat into advance.

If things are going well in your life, it is easy to dismiss the devil; but if you are going through a difficult patch, you may tend to back fearfully away. Your fear grows like a child in the dark. But whatever the state you are in, you must not succumb to fear of the demon, according to Ignatius. You must always react to his incursions with courage and bravery and he will slink away into the darkness like a frightened puppy. To quote Franklin D. Roosevelt's wife Eleanor:

> You gain strength, courage, and confidence by every experience in which you really stop to look fear in the face. You are able to say to yourself, 'I have lived through this horror. I can take the next thing that comes along.' You must do the thing you think you cannot do.

The second way the devil attacks is like a deceitful seducer who wants to keep his love affair secret and dreads being exposed. As John's Gospel points out, deceit is the language of the devil (John 8:44). He is like the man who tries to persuade the married woman he is seducing to keep his words and deeds hidden. If she divulges his dishonest talk and indecent designs to her husband, the deceitful seducer becomes exasperated and realizes he will not be able to succeed. In a similar way, the evil spirit who seduces you with his wiles also hopes that you will keep everything secret. If you reveal what is going on inside to a spiritual director, the devil loses heart for he realizes that his dark schemes have been brought into the light and he won't be able to fulfill his evil plans. The devil is in his element with secrecy and darkness, so it is vital to bring inner agitation and confusion transparently into the light with a fellow Christian who has spiritual knowledge and wisdom. The demon hates to be discovered and unmasked. Openness deprives him of his power.

The third typical tactic of the demon is to act like a military commander who examines the stronghold of his enemy and then attacks him where he is weakest (Ignatius' use of this analogy was undoubtedly influenced by his pre-conversion military experience). Saint Peter used a different image though the intent was similar: "Your enemy the devil prowls around like a roaring lion looking for someone to devour" (1 Peter 5:8). As a rule lions hunt by night, carefully stalking their prey, approaching them silently, and making their final charge from as little as 10 yards distance. Certain persons are so lacking in goodness and unconcerned about loving that they offer themselves as willing prey to the lion or leave their defenses completely open to the enemy commander. They make the devil's job easy. But the prey he really delights in hunting are the persons closest to God: these are the trophies for which he really exerts himself. The demon makes a thorough examination of their virtues. Then, in order to maximize his chances of success, he strikes where they are most vulnerable, or in a moment of loneliness or pain when their guard is down.

In order to be better prepared, it helps to grow in self-knowledge, to identify weaknesses and blind spots, and to work on them. Self-knowledge comes through introspection, but especially from the caring feedback of a trusted friend or the enlightened input of a spiritual counselor. But the most effective defense against the evil spirit is the disarming simplicity that comes from sustained contact with God: against the ingenuous heart of the true disciple of

Christ, even the vast intelligence and cunning of Satan are powerless. For instance there is a story told of a saintly monk who was visited one day by the devil, disguised as an angel of light. The devil began by saying, "I am the Angel Gabriel and I have been sent to you." But the humble monk, who had not the least trace of pride, simply replied, "You must have come to the wrong address. I have not done anything to deserve an angelic visitation." Defeated, the devil immediately departed.

If the devil were looking for an effective way to spread evil today, to gain unlimited access 24 hours a day into the minds and hearts of humanity, he would hardly need his prodigious intelligence to figure out that media, TV, the internet and so on offer ideal pathways. Now, please do not misunderstand me — I am not here to lament the world of the 21st century. I do not claim that TV and the internet are evil. As I said in the first chapter, evil is not a thing. Since TV and the internet are things, they are not of themselves evil. In fact, they are good and beneficial. Let me take an example from the worldwide web to clarify what I mean. Evil is analogous to a computer virus or worm: these are tiny pieces of software that piggyback on real programs and real computer networks in order to replicate and spread havoc worldwide. A computer virus cannot spread by itself. It needs to use a program or document as a platform. There are innumerable good computer programs, but the virus has the nasty ability to ruin them all.

In an analogous way, the evil spirit piggybacks the worldwide web. Like a virus, evil parasitically lives off this good thing, corrupting its goodness and distorting its truth with falsehood. It is because the web has such amazing capacities for good that it can be twisted so horrifically toward evil. The web makes it easier to do good: without leaving the keyboard, someone can donate money to charity or follow a guided prayer session on-line. But evil becomes frightfully easy to set in motion as well: through simply pointing and clicking a mouse, a gang fight can be planned, a suicide pact arranged, or pornography downloaded. As for TV, we unthinkingly allow it to bring people and situations into the intimacy of our living rooms that we would never allow enter our homes in real life. People callously torture and kill each other before our eyes, talk about and practice sex endlessly, utter all kinds of profanities, and we sit numbly there, our eyes glued to these ever-shifting images of vice and depravity. As the old Latin saying puts it, "The corruption of the best is the worst corruption" (*corruptio optimi pessima*). The best sources of information, education and communication can also become the worst when they are corrupted by the virus of evil.

We repeatedly experience the battle between good and evil interiorly. God draws us to what is noble, good, pure, and right. The evil spirit tries to sow doubt, anxiety, and despair. We cannot prevent negative thoughts and desires from popping up in consciousness, but we can decide what to do once they arrive. We need not be hospitable, we can politely and resolutely usher them out. We can enforce a policy of zero tolerance.

As we come to the close of this chapter, it is important to stress that even though I have devoted a lot of space to the wiles of the evil spirit, this is only in order to combat his insinuations, not with a view to exaggerate his significance. He remains a minor figure. There is only one God. And to become pure, we need to focus our attention exclusively on godly things: everything that is true, noble, right, pure, graceful, and exemplary (Philippians 4:8). This purifying diet is more than enough to enrich us immeasurably. We have to train ourselves to do this by prayer, reading God's word, and sharing our faith-vision together.

But we also need role models whose very lives uplift us and sweep us into God's loving orbit. That is why I now want to draw inspiration from a woman of pure love.

9

Pure Song

They overcame him by the blood of the Lamb and by the word of their testimony; they did not love their lives so much as to shrink from death. Therefore rejoice, you heavens and you who dwell in them!
The Book of Revelation 12:11-12.

Music the fiercest grief can charm,
And Fate's severest rage disarm:
Music can soften pain to ease,
And make despair and madness please:
Our joys below it can improve,
And antedate the bliss above.
Alexander Pope, "Ode for Music, on St. Cecilia's Day"

Musicians have composed in her honor, singers have beseeched her for inspiration, and artists have been ravished by her beauty. The greatest English poet before Shakespeare, Geoffrey Chaucer (c. 1340-1400), is one of a host of artists to have revered the ancient Roman martyr Cecilia. He listed five delightful meanings for her name in "The Second Nun's Prologue" to *The Canterbury Tales*. He took them directly from a medieval book full of stories of the saints called the *Golden Legend,* compiled by Jacobo di Voragine. Cecilia is the lily of heaven on account of her pure and virginal chastity. She is the path for the blind because of her example and teaching. She is contemplation and activity because of her unique blend of heavenly and earthly gifts. She lacks blindness because the radiant light of her wisdom and virtue shines. She is a heavenly sight because of her greatness.

But long before these creative spirits discovered her, countless Christians looked to Saint Cecilia as a model of purity. They loved her deeply and admired her greatly. She was immensely real for them and her story made a real difference to their lives. Who was she? What was she like? How did she live and how did she die?

Many historians believe the facts of Cecilia's life have been modified in the interests of a pious story. The account of Cecilia's marriage and martyrdom that is recounted in the fifth century Latin text, the "Passion of Saint Cecilia" [*Passio Sanctae Caeciliae*], lends credence to this view. It is hagiography in two senses: as well as being the biography of a saint, it idealizes Cecilia so much that the real woman is in danger of being edited out altogether.

But before we totally dismiss the hagiographical genre, it is important to remember that details are always altered to serve a life story. Imagine an account of someone's life that would aim for scrupulous precision of detail: "On the first Tuesday morning following the spring equinox Cecilia took a stroll at sunrise diagonally through the middle of her acre square garden bordered on each side by six fifteen foot high apple trees. Three birds were perched on the uppermost two branches of the first tree on her right, of which one, a male blackbird was in full song . . ." Even though such a record conveys minute details with great precision, it does not necessarily tell us much about the real life of the subject. Missing from the exact presentation just quoted, for example, are the face, voice, and figure of Cecilia, the complete woman who spiritually transformed so many lives. The living Cecilia is not there.

Not everything from a person's life can be inserted in a biography and not everything ought to be included. As with all biographies, a religious biography generally has a central theme, and the biographical details that are not of service to this theme do not survive in the written account. The short religious biography of Saint Cecilia handed down to us from the fifth century aims to highlight Cecilia's sanctity and edify readers. Unfortunately it makes her story stilted and ethereal in the process.

But there was nothing clichéd or forced about the passion with which Pope Paschal I scoured Rome for her mortal remains in 821, refusing to give up until he found her. Neither was there anything trite or threadbare in the festive way Cecilia was celebrated and honored centuries later in 1599 when her remains, having been lost a second time, were discovered yet again. (It is difficult to fathom how the Romans let her go once they had found her. To adapt Oscar Wilde's famous line — To lose a saint once may be regarded as a misfortune; to lose her twice looks like carelessness).

The saintly Pope Paschal I had a deep veneration for the Roman martyrs who were buried outside the city walls and ensured that the remains of many of them were moved into churches within the city. Assisted by no less than Cecilia herself who spoke to him in a vision, he found her miraculously incorrupt body hundreds of years after her death, lying in the precise posture described in the acts of her martyrdom. Her body, still preserved in all its purity as though she had fallen asleep, lay in the Catacombs of Saint Callistus on the Appian Way, in a small coffin. There were blood-soaked linen cloths at her feet. Paschal transferred her body, along with the remains of her husband Valerian and other companions, to the newly rebuilt church in Trastevere that he had constructed in her honor, a church believed to stand over the site of the house in which Cecilia once lived.

Over the course of centuries the exact location of her coffin was forgotten. She was found yet again during renovation work in the same church in Trastevere in 1599, wrapped in ornate fabrics supplied by Paschal, and still incorrupt. The discovery caused huge excitement in Rome, and enormous crowds filled the basilica. Pope Clement VIII joined over forty cardinals, including the future Saint Robert Bellarmine, and tens of thousands of lay people in venerating the beloved Cecilia. It was decided to preserve her image for future generations. Against all expert advice, the Church chose a young and untried artist to sculpt as exact a reproduction as possible for posterity. Stefano Maderno (1576-1636) selected a single block of Greek marble for his work. He was only 23 years of age when he set about creating this breathtaking piece, and never again did he fashion anything to rival the beauty of this statue.

Cecilia is shown lying on her right side, the legs bent at the knees and so somewhat contracted, the arms extended parallel to her body and slightly forwards, her left temple touching the ground with her head swiveled almost 180 degrees in what would be a natural position were she lying on her left side, but looks distinctly uncomfortable given the posture she is in. The long incision left by the triple blow to the back of her neck is clearly visible — no more than three strokes of the axe were allowed for the beheading of Roman citizens, and these had not been enough to sever Cecilia's neck, so she survived in a suffering state for three days, managing during that time to encourage other Christians, have her possessions distributed to the poor, as well as ensuring that a church would be built on the site of her house. Her husband Valerian, whom she had converted to the faith, had by this time suffered martyrdom along with his brother Tibertius. In his short life as a Christian, Valerian had brought Tibertius to God. By the time Cecilia was in the posture that Maderno sculpted for posterity, the extraordinary goals she set herself had been achieved and she was literally able to rest in peace.

Part of her face is covered with a veil and the rest of it is turned away from the viewer. The unexpected position of her head lends authenticity to the posture: it would be too uncomfortable a position for anyone to choose naturally. Having lost a lot of blood from the wound to her neck, Cecilia probably collapsed and fell in such a way that her head turned against its natural direction as it hit the ground, snapping the neck. In that moment of death she could no longer speak with her voice that had previously been pure song. But three of her fingers are reverently extended as though with her final exhalation she was still "witnessing" in line with the etymological meaning of the Greek word for "martyr," this time pointing adoringly to the sublime mystery of the Holy Trinity. And it was no accident either that her final suffering lasted exactly three days. Maderno engraved his own testimony at the foot of the statue: "Witness the body of the most holy virgin Cecilia whom I myself saw lying incorrupt in her tomb. In this marble I have expressed for you this very saint in exactly the same bodily posture." Maderno's sublime piece can still be seen under the main altar of the Basilica of Saint Cecilia in Trastevere, lying in a niche of black marble. The dark niche accentuates the shimmering radiance of his three-dimensional Cecilia.

The story of Saint Cecilia is not afraid of putting the gory truth before us — a woman who dies an agonizingly slow death, her lifeblood ebbing painfully away after a triple blow to the neck. And yet the light of glory radiates in that moment of unheralded victory, when the struggle is over and the prize is won. Her expiration is our inspiration. Broken open like a precious perfume, her essence rises and covers us like a fragrance. Its scent tells us that even the darkest moment will be transformed into pure light. On her wedding night Cecilia told her husband Valerian that she had an angel of God watching over her, and that he too would be able to see this heavenly being if he believed in the living and true God. We too could be graced with an awesome vision through the beauty of her witness.

Nobody is sure of the exact year of Cecilia's martyrdom. Estimations fluctuate wildly: some place it as early as 177, others as late as 362. I favor the year 230, mainly because Cecilia is traditionally linked with Pope Saint Urban who died in 230. Her tomb is in the Catacombs of Saint Callistus right next to the ancient crypt of the popes, which contains the remains of several pontiffs who died from the third decade of the third century onwards. This suggests that a date earlier than 230 is unlikely.

Unfortunately, the fifth century account of Cecilia imposes such a sanctimonious veneer on her marriage and martyrdom that the real woman is in danger of being asphyxiated beneath. Under the pious wrappings there is a great story struggling to break free, like Michelangelo's unfinished slaves who seem to move and writhe in the labor to liberate themselves from their blocks of marble.

But there are two happenings in this pious story that ring especially true: Cecilia's marriage and the moment of her death. The "Passion of Saint Cecilia" is so otherwise formulaic that her consent to marry a pagan strikes the reader as rash and reckless. It breaks the mold with an almighty clatter. There was no precedent for this: Christian women before Cecilia's time who were set on virginity preferred to die rather than marry pagans and compromise their vow. The capacity to conjure this scenario out of thin air would have exceeded the pedestrian imagination of the fifth century author. This extraordinary wedding day has a ring of authenticity about it. But it is not just her wedding that surprises; Cecilia also dies in an unexpected manner. Her end has not the drama of a bright and burning comet; instead she flickers on and off in her final days, like an uncertainly glowing ember.

Looking at her life from the outside and from the distance of centuries, we can only capture fragments of its greatness. Like Jacob struggling with the angel, we always emerge limp and lame in the struggle to portray the dazzling fullness of a saintly life. Yet the tragic glory of her story can gift us with a new vision. It is worth trying to imagine our way into it. A certain amount of poetic license is called for — but in the case of a saint so beloved of poets, it may just be permissible.

Let us say that Cecilia was born into a noble Roman family about 212 and brought up a Christian. By this time

Christianity had been embraced by important figures among the Roman aristocracy, though there was still a deep-rooted suspicion of this foreign faith, exemplified by the edict of Septimus Severus in 202 which imposed heavy penalties on those Romans who converted to Christianity or Judaism. Her parents would have vividly remembered the severe persecution of Christians during the nineteen-year reign of the philosopher emperor Marcus Aurelius. They would have been relieved too at the partial respite that followed during the twelve-year reign of his strange son Commodus.

As she grew up Cecilia became aware that a new Rome had sprung up imperceptibly around her — not the great empire whose power extended throughout the known world, but the invisible and hidden Rome founded on the blood of the great apostles Peter and Paul. She prayed at the tomb of Saint Peter on the hill of the Vatican, heartened by the humility of the apostle who, feeling unworthy of his master, asked to be crucified with his head downwards. She prayed too at the tomb along the via Ostia that held the remains of one of the most dynamic saints of all time, the apostle Paul, also executed toward the end of Nero's reign.

The Roman catacombs, a vast network of underground galleries in which the early Christians buried their dead, were relatively new during Cecilia's lifetime. The first catacombs, many taking their names from noble families such as Priscilla and Domitilla who owned the properties, only began to be constructed fifty years or so before her birth. The systematic enlargement of these subterranean honeycombs that began to take place during Cecilia's lifetime was made possible by generous donations from wealthy families like her own. Like any child, Cecilia was fascinated by this dark underground world containing the bodies of so many

Christians who had fallen asleep. She sometimes had the chance to descend below ground and walk in procession with other Christians along the cold corridors carved out of tuff, the volcanic rock found all over Rome. Her eyes feasted on the symbols and wall painting that their torches lit up — the figure of the Good Shepherd, the lamb held across his shoulders, his powerful hands tightly clasped around the legs of the bleating animal; the Greek word for fish, *ichthus*, also an acronym for "Jesus Christ God's Son Savior" (*Iesos Christos Theou Huios Soter*); the dove holding an olive branch in its beak. She wondered at these cryptic symbols which depicted key Christian doctrines and beliefs.

"Wonder is the feeling of the lover of wisdom and the love of wisdom begins in wonder," writes Plato in his *Theaetetus* and Aristotle notes in the first book of his *Metaphysics* that although wonder is initially aroused by trivial things, it goes on to focus on deeper matters. As Cecilia gazed at the catacombs, her spirit began to breathe more fully. She saw the resting places of martyrs stacked along these dark and meandering galleries. In the midst of awful sufferings, they had already sung glad hosannas in anticipation of heaven. She prayed for the grace to face death with such joyful assurance. She already glimpsed the light beyond the darkness, the voice beyond the silence of the tomb, the Word of God who murmured loving words in her heart. She too wanted to die loving the God who had died in love for her.

Cecilia began to see beyond the rupture of death to the rapture, beyond the break between this world and the next to the continuity between them. She knew that by being a friend of God on earth she would also be his friend in heaven. By desiring God fully in the now she would find this desire fulfilled beyond all expectations later. Anticipating those final heartbeats, she played out a dress rehearsal in her heart: what did she want to say to God at that final and defining moment? What feelings did she want to express? She practised her speech over and over and sensed that God took up her words of love and stored them for the future where they would ease her passage into true life. She resolved to face death with absolute faith and complete bravery: she wanted to utter the greatest proof of her love with her last breath, with the exaltation of her final exhalation.

Death would be the birthday of her new life: like her fellow Christians of the time, Cecilia liked to call the day of death *dies natalis*, literally, the day of birth. It would be the moment she always longed for: to meet God face to face. She loved God and longed to enter his presence. She nourished the desire of imitating the great cloud of Christian witnesses by one day laying down her own life. In the meantime she made a secret vow of virginity to give permanent expression to the fact that she had fallen in love with God.

Cecilia had often walked through the Roman Forum, pausing in front of the magnificent Temple of the Vestal Virgins. These six self-sacrificing women were highly prized in the city. What Cecilia liked most about them was not the fact that they had special seats at banquets and the games. No, what she really warmed to was the power of their compassion. If a condemned prisoner met a vestal virgin on his way to execution, he was granted an immediate pardon. She had once seen such a prisoner being dragged in chains along a dirt road, whipped intermittently by his captors, a haggard look on his face, more brute than man. And then a regal carriage appeared in view. It slowed down to a halt. A beautiful woman in long flowing robes alighted. As the guards stood to attention, the prisoner squinted disbelievingly, and then threw himself to the ground, mumbling incomprehensibly in the dirt. Cecilia and the other onlookers held their breath. The vestal virgin stretched forth her arm. "Set him free," she cried imperiously. The bewildered prisoner remained kneeling in the dust, smiling in a confused and innocent way as the guards undid his chains.

One of the vestal virgins had been a childhood friend of Cecilia, born like her of a patrician family. But at the age of 7 she became a novice, and began her thirty years of service. Now she preserved the undying fire that was sacred to Vesta, the goddess of heath and home. But Cecilia wanted to go further. Thirty years were too short for her. She wanted to promise virginity forever. The spirit of conquest that ran in her aristocratic blood and veins took a new turn with this girl. It was the reign of God she wanted to spread, it was love that she wanted to see conquering all. She intuitively knew that the strength of her love would be proportionate to the greatness of her sacrifice.

Like any lover, Cecilia continually thought of her beloved. She was swept away by the beauty of God, delighting in his amazing attributes, pondering his astounding goodness, and thanking him for dying out of love for her. She always carried the Gospels hidden on her person, reading and re-reading them in order to get to know God ever more deeply, so that she could love him and serve him better. She knew these writings were inspired, and she was gladly inspired to read them. Through these words she heard God's voice speaking to her in the depths of her heart.

Cecilia was fortunate to find a great spiritual director, Pope Saint Urban I, who reigned from 222 to 230. Urban's goodness was so radiant that the number of Christians increased dramatically during his pontificate. His very appearance communicated holiness. Urban was an old man when Cecilia first met him. He reminded her of another old man she had read about in Homer's *Odyssey*, the wise and willing guide called Mentor. Once Mentor had come up to Odysseus' son Telemachus and said, "if you are made of the same stuff as your father, you will be neither foolish nor cowardly." The more Cecilia learned from Urban, the more she found that the "stuff" of her heavenly Father, his grace, was making her into someone new and fearless.

Her family was proud of Cecilia and of her beauty. But it was inner beauty she cultivated. She was not at ease in noble surroundings and sumptuous settings. She craved simplicity. She craved God. Through obedience to her parents she dressed in splendid clothes of gold. But underneath she always wore a penitential under-garment. In her early teenage years she had managed to hold out against marriage despite the pressure of her parents. But now she was 18, and time had run out. There had been a line of patrician suitors queuing up for years. Her parents had just chosen their favorite, a young nobleman of integrity and honor. His name was Valerian and he was deeply in love with her. Her parents approved and saw the advantages of a union between these two illustrious families. They knew nothing of her secret vow of virginity.

Neither was Valerian aware of Cecilia's vow. He expected a sexual relationship as part of their marriage. The time of trial had arrived for the teenage girl as it does for all saints. If she consented to this marriage there seemed no way to preserve her virginity but if she refused she would disobey her parents. Wasn't it nonsensical to agree to marriage since she had made a perpetual vow of virginity? It was going against everything she had committed herself to. And God could not possibly require her to acquiesce to Valerian. It was God who had drawn her away from thoughts of marriage in the first place by whisperings words of love in her heart. Cecilia was adamant that the God in whom she believed would not demand the sacrifice of her virginity. Was it all a devilish temptation? Was the evil spirit intent on destroying the precious gift of body and soul that she had so generously given to God?

She loved her parents but she realized they had a human way of seeing things: they wanted the best for her in terms of prestige and status. They wanted to secure her material future. The voice of the evil spirit tempted her to disobedience, suggesting that God would be only too happy to excuse her from obeying parents who did not know about her vow. They were guided by nothing more than worldliness in their notions of true greatness. Doubts began to sprout in her mind. Weren't her father and mother all too human? A vapor of pride insinuated itself — weren't they unworthy to be parents of a saintly girl like herself? Cecilia said a resolute "no" to these temptations, for her best instincts told her to obey her parents and not to make a mini-goddess of herself. Urban confirmed that obedience always saves, and reassured her that she could count on God to defend her honor.

But Cecilia herself went beyond even the daring faith that Urban proposed. Her faith blossomed in this time of trial. She was bold enough to begin to believe not only for herself but also for Valerian. She sensed that God would not only protect her from harm and guard her virginity, but through her would also win Valerian over to Christianity. She expected the impossible from God. As the wedding day approached, Cecilia sang a song in her heart, asking God to maintain her virginity and make it spiritually fertile. She fasted for three days, praying continually. With prayer she nourished her deepest desire, which was for God; with fasting she let go of lesser desires that were not directed toward God. She told her body that Jesus was Lord of her life. She felt a new readiness to surrender everything. Even though physically weak, she sensed God's strength. Because she was empty, she could become full of God. But her fasting was above all for Valerian. She knew from the Gospels she held close to her heart that some spirits are only cast out by prayer and fasting. Prayer alone could not rid Valerian of his sensual desires and his attachment to paganism. But fasting combined with prayer would work wonders and break down walls that would never topple otherwise. She prayed to the angel whom God had put at her side to encourage and protect her. Cecilia also confidently turned to the saints, especially to the Virgin Mary, for Mary had remained a virgin despite being given in marriage to Joseph.

She felt an unwavering conviction when the day of marriage arrived. She was sure that with God on her side she could achieve what was humanly impossible. She was certain that she would remain a virgin. She was confident that she would be given the power to move the mountain of paganism that inhabited her husband. The future was going to work out for the best. She did not demand a sign that prayer was successful. She did not ask for postponement of the marriage. She had an inner proof that did not need to be buttressed by outward evidence. At the same time she knew she was entering uncharted territory. There was the real risk that her husband would attack and even kill her if she refused to go to bed with him. No woman she knew had found herself in such a situation. Yet she was without fear. She did not feel alone. God was with her and he had placed an angel at her side.

Valerian had no idea what was going on inside his bride. He was simply entranced by her. At the wedding ceremony he was impressed by her dignity and serenity, unaware that she was in continual silent prayer. He noticed that she ate little during the sumptuous banquet that followed. Once the last guests had departed and he was alone with his wife, the moment for which he had been waiting finally arrived. This was the evening he had dreamt about for so long, the first night of their life together. Cecilia was everything he had ever wanted in a woman. It was not just her beauty, but it was also that. He was in awe of her goodness; he noticed how she treated everyone with respect and always put others before herself. He found her enchanting and mysterious as well: often she gazed dreamily into the distance with an ecstatic expression on her face. He wanted to know her more, he wanted to penetrate her mystery. He felt an incredible sense of peace and joy whenever she was around. He could not imagine himself loving any other woman. And now at last he had the opportunity to give physical expression to the desires that burned within him.

Valerian was ignorant of her vow of virginity; he did not even know she was a Christian. He had heard rumors that she was a member of this superstitious cult with its half-baked prejudices, but had immediately dismissed the idea as unworthy of her. Marriages between Christians and pagans were not uncommon at that time. But if a Christian woman married a man who had no understanding or tolerance for her religion, it proved almost impossible for her to practice it: he would immediately became suspicious if she asked to join other Christians in night prayer vigils or took off to the poor part of town to feed the hungry and clothe the naked.

Valerian felt the cool evening air waft through the window as he stood facing his bride in the large bedroom. He smiled at her and she smiled back. He reached out his hands and motioned her toward the bridal bed. She remained stuck to the spot.

Valerian was taken aback, but quickly reasoned that this was only feigned coyness. He went to embrace her, "Come Cecilia, I love you so much."

"And I love you as well, but not in the way you imagine," she replied, withdrawing a few steps.

"But you're my wife!" he exclaimed.

"Valerian, I am married to God. I am a Christian. Like the angels I serve God. And right now there is an angel standing at my side to defend me. If you want to avoid his wrath, do not lay a hand on me."

"Let's finish the fun and games, shall we?" Valarian said, angrily. "And don't start telling me you're a Christian! With your beauty and goodness, you couldn't possibly lower yourself to the level of that disgusting rabble."

"It's true Valerian. I am a Christian: it is the joy of my life, and it will be an even greater joy in the next life. And I love you so much that I want you to meet God as well."

Valerian began to pace up and down the room in anger, before shouting, "Can't you see that with one blow, I could smash your skull to smithereens!"

Cecilia looked at him bravely and trustingly. "But you're not that kind of man, Valerian. You're good and loving. You have been from the first moment we met. You would never attack me for speaking the truth."

"Truth! How can this be truth? First you tell me your angel is standing next to you, and then you say you want to introduce me to your God. But all I see here is you, me and that bed. If you want truth, here it is: a few hours ago you promised to be my wife, and part of that promise means going to bed with me — in case you happened to forget. Now, that's the truth I believe in, not some drivel about an invisible angel who is going to strike me down if I try to touch my own wife."

"Valerian, how can you doubt me? As you say, with one blow you could kill me and yet you see that I am not afraid, for my angel is present."

"If you want me to believe what you say," said Valerian, his tone softening slightly, "then just do me one favor — let me see this angel of yours."

Cecilia paused for a second and Valerian half-expected her to summon the angel. Instead she said, "If you want to see the angel, believe as I do." Her hand moved quickly to her heart and she took out a tiny scroll, opening the twenty-eighth chapter of Matthew's Gospel. "These are the words of God, words I always carry next to me. I know I can rely on them because God only speaks the truth. See what is written here: the angel tells the women not to be afraid because Jesus has conquered death, just as he promised. Death no longer has power over us."

"But how can you say that? You Christians die just like everyone else. In fact, you don't even live as long as we do.

171

Rome has lost count of the number of Christians who have been thrown to the wild beasts."

"But we don't die. We live. We live in a paradise that surpasses anything you could possibly imagine. Oh, if only you could picture the joy of losing your voice amidst the choirs of thousands of angels singing songs to ravish your heart, touching the chords of your spirit as they chant God's unfathomable love! Lord, I join my voice with theirs, I sing for Valerian, my beloved husband, give him your love, may we love you as one, may we one day sing in harmony before your throne!"

Valerian, genuinely moved, fixed his eyes on her admiringly. He had always been in love with her, but at this moment he saw a quality in her face that he had never seen before, something he could not grasp but strangely felt willing to die for. "Cecilia, I don't know what it is you've got; all this is new to me. But I know you have something special and whatever it is, I want to share in it. I want to believe in your God. I want to be like you, if only your God could accept someone like me?"

"My God has always wanted to accept you, to welcome you with open arms, to embrace you tenderly. If you only knew how much my God loves you, how much he wants to be your God, how much he wants to crown your life with joy . . ." She looked at him imploringly with her candid eyes.

Valerian felt unexpected tears well up in his eyes. He caught a glimpse of a world that he could not see clearly, but whose existence he could not deny. At the same time he knew that in comparison with Cecilia's dignity and depth, his own life had only skated the surface.

Cecilia opened another passage, this time from the Gospel of John, drew Valerian to her, put one arm in his and holding the scroll with the other, began to read in an unforgettable voice that sounded like song, "For God so loved the world that he gave his one and only Son, that whoever believes in him shall not perish but have eternal life. For God did not send his Son into the world to condemn the world, but to save the world through him . . ." Valerian listened, motionless at first, grateful yet unsure. He could hear echoes from somewhere else in her melodious voice. As she continued, he began to nod, looking from her to the scroll and back again. His needling fear lost its sharpness, flooded by an exhilarating surge. He had doubts as he thought of the life he was leaving behind, yet he was strengthened immeasurably by her faith.

At this point we leave the story of Cecilia and extract two lessons from its depth: her vulnerability and her purity. Cecilia had the valor of a defenseless heart. She walked fearlessly into marriage with a pagan husband, confident that he would become Christian. She was not disheartened at her powerlessness; she paid no attention to the peril she was in because her eyes were fixed solely on God. In the midst of darkness she saw light, in the threatening shadows she glimpsed rays of the Divine Sun. She herself became the flame of a candle that drew Valerian's gaze upwards: "I no longer live but Christ lives in me" (Galatians 2:20). Cecilia let Jesus dwell within her in such a luminous manner that Jesus drew Valerian to himself through Cecilia.

Cecilia's fragility is evoked too by her debilitating state after the botched attempt to behead her, when she lay in a pool of her own blood for three days, in an echo of Good Friday, Holy Saturday and Easter Sunday. Maderno's 1599 statue shows her laid bare in all her vulnerability, her broken and wounded body lying mutely upon the earth at the moment of death. Her body still looks warm and the garment wrapped around her is softly draped. She does not scream. She is shrouded in silence like the veil that envelops her. She possesses the inviolate dignity of a warrior who has given her last drop of blood for the noblest of endeavors. Although the quality of Cecilia's life is physically impoverished, the statue suggests the extraordinary richness of the life of her soul. "For when I am weak, then I am strong" (2 Corinthians 12:10). There is no fretfulness or fear in Cecilia, there is no dread or dismay; in her suffering there is serenity. She has no shame in her weakness; instead she is filled with grandeur, proclaiming God's power with her whole being — a power that reaches to her very fingertips, which indicate the Trinity.

God has the surprising habit of working through our weaknesses, and not our strengths. God did not work through Cecilia because she happened to be one of the most eligible noblewomen of Rome. God worked through her because she did not rely on her privilege or position, her beauty or charm, but confided in the power of God instead. The truth is that when we think we can do everything, we really do nothing useful, because we do it on our own. "No man is an island," and when we cut ourselves off from God, our mainland, we fail. If we are full of ourselves, we cannot be filled with the Spirit. If we make a god of ourselves, our self-directed idolatry leaves no space for the living God to enter.

But when we accept our powerlessness, God's power can take over. And when that happens, we do things we never imagined and that others cannot guess at either. If

Cecilia had been able to speak at the moment of death, she would have shocked listeners with her overflowing gratitude to God for this new-found weakness: "This is it! Now that I am at my lowest ebb, I rely on God as never before." From a human point of view, the ravaged wasteland that her body had become should have eroded her self-confidence and toppled her into the abyss. But she was strengthened interiorly by a power unrivalled anywhere on heaven or earth. And when God worked through her vulnerability, it was obviously God's work, not hers. Her soul drifted away from her body and her life moved beyond the earth, but she was never for a moment abandoned by God. In the darkness of death, her light shone all the more.

Cecilia's pure light was also an enlivening fire. Through fire everything becomes transformed, and Cecilia had burned away the inessentials of life with the fire of purity. In her own city, the vestal virgins preserved the sacred fire at the shrine of Vesta. To keep the fire alight demanded continual attention on their part. If the fire went out, it was evidence that the vestals had become impure, and this threatened the well-being of all Rome, spelling disaster for the city. Cecilia jealously guarded the fire of her love, like the angel and flaming sword guarding the entrance to the tree of life (Genesis 3:24). She did not allow the tumultuous events of her life to distance her from this saving fire. She kept stoking it so that it would not flicker and die. Again and again she threw into the fire her love of God, her desire to do great things for him, her care for those around her, her little and big sacrifices, her sufferings and joys. And consequently the fire became red hot, warming the lives of those around her.

Cecilia sang a great song. However our task is not to live her life or borrow her lines, but to find our own song. It can take some false notes before we get the pitch right. We need the gift of discernment to help us. In one of his final poems, "The Circus Animals' Desertion," William Butler Yeats (1865-1939) describes his fruitless search for a poetic theme. And while doing so, he reminisces over his life, and realizes that a lot of what he wrote was only for show, surface without depth. Before old age mercilessly stripped him of illusions, he was able to fool himself but now he knows better. Although his images often attained a great purity, they started from the ordinariness and even messiness of "old kettles, old bottles, and a broken can." In order to be authentic he confesses that he must return to where every ladder begins: "the foul rag and bone shop of the heart." Yeats was referring to the kind of Irish village shop that sold discarded rags and bones which could be used as a cheap type of fertilizer by gardeners and farmers. Although the rags and bones smelt pretty foul, the herbs and flowers that bloomed as a result were beautiful, radiating pure and invigorating fragrances.

Nobody smells pretty in the morning, and no one feels particularly angelic when the alarm clock goes off. Yet we human beings can combine the earthiness of animals with the spirit of angels, because we occupy a unique position in the universe, being both thoroughly physical and highly spiritual. Our flesh is real and visible; our spirits, even though they are invisible and never register on weighing scales, are no less real.

Angels seem utterly beyond us. Although they are creatures, they are vastly superior to us. After all, despite the often significant differences between human individuals, we nevertheless all belong to the one species — the human species. But angels are so unique that each belongs to its own species. Each angel comprises a species of one. Consequently, the individuality and personality of angels is much more perfect and sophisticated than anything we know. Because of this, every angel manifests a completely new facet to the infinite richness of God. And angels transcend us in so many other ways — through their unceasing love, their perfect purity, complete serenity, and vast intelligence.

And yet despite their wonderful perfection, angels are inferior to human beings in one crucial respect: unlike Cecilia, no angel can sacrifice himself in imitation of Christ, no angel can express his love as Cecilia did by laying down her life. "Greater love has no one than this, that he lay down his life for his friends." (John 15:13). No angel has greater love than this self-sacrificing love. But in order to live that kind of altruistic love, we humans need to become pure. Otherwise, such love will never attract us.

To ascend the ladder to heaven, we must start from where we find ourselves on the earth. In the Book of Genesis, Jacob dreams of a ladder leading from earth to heaven, full of angels ascending and descending (Genesis 28:12). Only angels freely move up and down the ladder. Angels are pure and purity makes this astonishing mobility possible. The ladder of pure love has union with God at one end and service of human beings at the other. Like the angels ascending and descending, it is essential to embrace both God and humanity. If one of these key elements is missing, there is no ladder, and we are rendered immobile.

Not everyone is especially holy, but everyone can have a special holiness when it comes to their own lives. Most of us will not become martyrs like Cecilia, or exude the joy of Francis of Assisi, but each of us can express our goodness in small ways — in daily work and in relationships. However mundane this love seems, it can make us great. It is important not to get discouraged by confusing quantity and quality when it comes to love. In fact, love is not about doing an enormous amount of things. Instead it is about doing whatever we do, however insignificant, with great love. Each of us has something unrivalled to offer to God: ourselves. If our desire marries with God's desire, there is nothing that we cannot achieve together. But for that to happen we need to believe in love. Then our lives will be transformed in the most astounding way. To love is to give the best of ourselves, not the worst. And when we truly love we are sharing something greater than ourselves — God, because God is true love.

Love makes us beautiful inside with a radiance that spreads to all around us, inspiring and moving others to do good in their turn — *bonum est diffusivum sui* ("good is diffusive of itself") as the Latin maxim puts it. If we could start by giving our souls at least as much care as our bodies, we would have already made a wonderful advance. Singing our own song is the greatest victory we will ever achieve. But only the daring win.

Afterword: Adoration

You are worthy, our Lord and God, to receive glory and honor and power.

Revelation 4:11

You have made me so rich, oh God, please let me share out Your beauty with open hands. My life has become an uninterrupted dialogue with You, oh God, one great dialogue.

Etty Hillesum, "Letter from Westerbrook", 18 August 1943

This afterword is intended to stay with you and most of all with me afterwards. It is not an afterword in the sense of a superfluous or redundant word. Rather it is a central and an indispensable word. I hope it abides long after many of the other words written here have been lost from memory. Although the last word, it is also the first, because it is the fundamental stance of the creature before the Creator, of the adopted child before the heavenly Father. The word is "adoration." It is the human response to God's utter purity, unimaginable holiness and transcendent perfection. There is not the slightest taint of impurity in God. He is free of all defilement. Adoration is the loving avowal and jubilant

179

recognition of God's holiness. Adoration is above all an internal act of the mind and the will: inside us God's holiness glows before the light of our minds and consequently, through adoration, we freely choose to glorify and worship God in his ineffable goodness. But adoration is not only interior; it also manifests itself outwardly. Because we are creatures of flesh and blood, we cannot but physically express the awe and worship that flood our hearts. Adoration is so deep-rooted and passionate that it spills over into physical postures of reverence and vocal expressions of heartfelt praise. And these physical outpourings of adoration in turn irrigate the interior fountain from which they rise, enabling it to gush forth more generously. Adoration is total: I do not adore with only part of my heart, with merely a few fibers of my being, with what is left over. I adore with my whole self.

Adoration is reflected in the gift of the fear of the Lord. The fear of the Lord is not stifling or suffocating, it is not alarming or asphyxiating, it is not a fear that disturbs or debilitates us, it does not upset or upend us, it does not lead to panic or paralyze. The fear of the Lord is a gift of the good Spirit, the Holy Spirit. It fills us with reverence and respect before God, with awe and admiration at his unimaginable goodness, with heartfelt humility in the face of his holiness. The gift of the fear of the Lord illuminates our own abyss of nothingness before the infinite love of God. It entails wakefulness and watchfulness but never sinks into dejection. We feel our littleness and weakness, yet cling to our confidence in God's inexhaustible love. We hate to offend God, yet when we fall we trustingly ask God to help us rise again and continue our journey, never doubting his loving help.

The phrase "the fear of the Lord" can be misleading: it is not a question of being afraid of God in the sense of being fearful of giving ourselves to him; neither is it a matter of slavish submission to a capricious sovereign. Instead it means a deeply-held awe that will only become more profound in the next life, a sense of wondrous astonishment that we are even his sons and daughters in the first place. We fear most of all the uncaring and selfish parts of ourselves, and it is most of all God whom we can allow ourselves to trust, for he will help us. In the face of God's incomparable goodness, we feel sorry for our sins with a sorrow that purifies but does not sadden us, for it is always allied to immense confidence in God's mercy, and such winning trust brings joy.

As I was finishing this book, I looked over some notes I made during a recent 30 day experience of silent prayer and fasting. And I remembered again what I had been in danger of forgetting — that adoration was the guiding motif of that privileged month-long encounter with God. And it also dawned on me that adoration is umbilically linked with becoming pure. The many hours I spent silently before the tabernacle, gazing at the body of Christ, began to disinfect my body, purify my soul and perfect my way of looking. Here are some of the notes from those privileged weeks that I have collated and edited.

The scent of pine is so powerful I can taste it as I cycle along the forest path. The innumerable slender trees look like an endless succession of stretched and elongated legs. To my right the River Havel sparkles in the sun. I descend towards a large red brick house that looks out onto the water. A white-haired old man leaning on his Zimmer frame looks up, squinting hard. I wave and shout "*Guten Tag Pater*" as I fly past. I park the bicycle and walk a few yards to the river's edge. A Polish barge passes by, its engine chugging contentedly, and the pungent smell of coal fills the air. The river swells on either side of the vessel and waves slap against the low wall that separates the garden from the water.

Jesus spent forty days praying and fasting in an unappealing spot by the Dead Sea. It was an arid expanse of parched earth leading down to a stagnant lake that looked like a pool of petrol and sucked the life out of the land around it. Here and there were isolated tufts of grass and short thorny bushes, but most of all there was dirty grey sand and unremitting rock.

Where I am is more like Galilee. The grass is green and thick, growing in lush meadows, there are rose bushes and flower-beds, rivers, lakes, and trees. I am in the middle of Germany. The choice of Germany for this lengthy period of silence, prayer and fasting has dented my spiritual credibility among hipper friends. If I were in Tibet, they would feel a lot better. Yet Germany makes sense. I studied German in college and spent an enjoyable semester reading theology at the University of Münster, where it rained even more frequently than in Ireland. I like Germans. They exhibit refreshing idealism and true depth, and once you break through the reserved exterior they turn into affectionate and loyal friends. Granted, their language leaves a lot to be desired. In his hilarious essay "The Awful German Language," Mark Twain deliciously describes some of its more ludicrous features:

The word *Schlag* means Blow, Stroke, Dash, Hit, Shock, Clap, Slap, Time, Bar, Coin, Stamp, Kind, Sort, Manner, Way, Apoplexy, Wood-cutting, Enclosure, Field, Forest-clearing. This is its simple and *exact* meaning — that is to say, its restricted, fettered meaning; but there are ways by which you can set it free, so that it can soar away, as on the wings of the morning, and never be at rest. You can hang any word you please to its tail, and make it mean anything you want to. You can begin with *Schlag-ader*, which means artery, and you can hang on the whole dictionary, word by word, clear through the alphabet to *Schlag-wasser*, which means bilge-water — and including *Schlag-mutter*, which means mother-in-law.

However awful the language, I am happily immersed in it, less than 20 miles from Berlin, on the banks of the River Havel, all the while wondering why nobody told me the hinterland of the German capital was so beautiful. Not only is the landscape much better than I expected; the people do not conform to the Prussian stereotype. They are relaxed, friendly and laugh easily. The house is near the village of Kladow, situated at the furthermost point of former West Berlin. After Communist East Germany encircled West Berlin, Kladow was as far as West Berliners could go for a weekend stroll. The border ran through the river in front of the house, and between August 1961 and November 1989, when the Berlin Wall eventually came down, people were mercilessly shot dead trying to cross the water.

When I arrived here in August, I did experience culture shock. There are 20 elderly and infirm Jesuits living in the retreat house complex. Having no immediate plans for becoming old, I was not sure how I would cope. But confounding all my fears, they have turned out to be a delightful bunch. Many of them are living examples that gracefulness and old age are not mutually exclusive.

I get an e-mail from my friend Norbert in Stockholm — "30 days of silence! Man, I just couldn't hack that." The question is: can I? Will I be able to keep my mouth shut for that long? And presuming that I do, will I go mad in the process? Will it all be too much for me? Will I start blabbering to the birds one fine morning? Francis of Assisi spoke to them out of love; I may easily do so out of desperation.

One day to go before the odyssey begins. Brother Eric, who takes care of the practical affairs of the house, has nailed a plank into a wooden girder under the ceiling of the colonnaded corridor in the outer courtyard, in order to support a swallow's nest. Inside the nest are three baby swallows. They have grown enormously over the last several days. Now they barely manage to nestle side by side in their tiny living space. Their mother swoops under the colonnade every ten minutes in a blazing blur of color and three big red mouths open wider than I thought possible. The mother hovers next to them. Within a couple of seconds she has fed each one and flown away again. But today when I go to look at the little swallows, all that is left is the small nest above the plank, and the large mass of droppings on the ground underneath, evidence of the weeks they have fed there. Now they are flying free.

This time of prayer is a pilgrimage with God, an invitation to deeper freedom. I cultivate outer silence in the hope that the inner noise will also abate enough to allow me to hear God's voice within. Ignatius of Loyola realized that much knowledge does not satisfy the soul; only tasting things deeply fills it. The heart of these weeks will be in tasting, savouring, loving Jesus. I ask him to let me know him more so that I can love him better and follow him more closely.

I am looking forward to this, and feel extremely lucky that I have been given the time to do it. Heaven is about being with God, and it helps to start working intensively on the relationship in advance. I am grateful to so many people who are praying for me. I feel like a child about to enter a shop stocked with goodies, or an underwater explorer on the brink of diving into a deep ocean filled with all sorts of fish, sea creatures, and exotic plants that bend and flex with the water. Or maybe I am walking by a serene lake where I expect to see elegant swans with snow-white wings and immaculate plumage, floating with graceful effortlessness, coyly slipping their heads and supple necks beneath the folds of their wings.

The big question: What do I fundamentally want out of this month? The answer that surges within is disarmingly simple: I want to adore God. I want to be nothing before him, just a grain of incense that burns and becomes a perfume ascending to his throne. I cannot articulate everything I desire, because what I want is more than I can know. So I will put it this way: I want to be everything God wants me to be.

I am on my knees on the carpeted floor of the chapel. I incline my head downwards. I ask various saints, known and lesser known, for help. I have a long list of these influential friends: I begin by asking the Virgin Mary to be with me. Then I turn to Saint Joseph. Among the apostles, I think particularly of John, Peter, James and Thomas. From the first female disciples Mary of Magdalene comes especially to mind. From the early Christian martyrs, Cecilia; Ignatius of Loyola, of course, and many others; last but certainly not least, my guardian angel. I touch the carpet with my forehand as I adore the Trinity. I ask the Holy Spirit to fill me with love, to carry me along the road to the fullness of love.

A succession of images play on the cinema screen of my mind. I see a swan, pure and white, shy and elegant. I want to love you like that. I see a cheetah racing through the African steppes. I want my love to be that hungry for you. A falcon drops like a bullet from the sky. Yes with that speed! A spider's web embroidered against a clear window pane: with that finesse and delicacy. Hundreds of birds rising from trees suddenly into the air, wings flapping in perfect synchronicity: with that spellbinding harmony. A bolt of lightning flashing across the dark sky: with that energy. Virgin snow on a remote glacier: with that purity. The deep ocean: with that depth. The rippling smiling water of a lake sparkling as it mirrors the sun: with that charm. A laughing dolphin leaping and dancing over the waves: with that joyful exuberance. The deep sound of a pealing bell in a monastery: with that tranquil voice. Thousands of Muslim worshippers prostrated in prayer: with that reverence. A comet racing across the heavens, shedding continual light: with that happy expense of myself. A black hole swallowing everything: where everything becomes you. Planets orbiting around the sun: centered on you. An ant tugging a burden twice its weight over the sand and pebbles: carrying everything for you. A bee laden with honey: giving you the sweetest of myself. I want to love you like the noblest of minds, like the most loving of hearts, "to the depth and breadth and height my soul can reach" (Elisabeth Barrett Browning).

I see myself as a tiny speck in the middle of space, surrounded by a vast flux of elements: exploding stars, planets near and far, quarks, bursts of energy, trails of light. And this speck, this particle of dust that is almost nothing utterly adores the majesty of the almighty and loving God. Today is the birthday of the Blessed Virgin Mary. I feel the Spirit gifted me with these joyful images on this feast of hers, snapshots of the joy her goodness brought to God. And I am astonished at her desiring heart, yearning for the Messiah, thirsting for his arrival, spending herself in prayer, sighing with expectation, the words of the psalms singing in her soul, lines from the Scripture welling up within her. I thank God for this hour of dynamism, energy and abundance. I thank God for his generosity to this nothing as I bow my head once more to the ground.

I take the old rowing boat out in the late afternoon and row around "*Pfaueninsel*" or Peacock Island which is about 150 yards across the River Havel from our house. Water hens scuttle into the tall reeds as the oars splash in the water. Half-way around the island a prim wooden bridge appears by the shore. A couple of storks eye me warily. As I come to the narrowest strait that separates the island from the mainland, a small ferry pulls away from the jetty and heads all of 30 yards across to the island. The water in the distance is as still as a mirror. A shiny neo-Gothic palace comes into view between the trees and I pass by several anchored cruise boats as I head back towards our house. My prayer is like rowing the boat around the island: I am circling a mystery that I cannot fathom, and seeing hints of a glory that I cannot imagine from where I find myself now.

Scores of swallows have gathered around the eaves of the infirmary, flying at breathtaking angles and in all directions, stopping regularly to land on the tiled roof. I see a few flying under the arch and threading their way rapidly between the colonnades of the courtyard — perhaps the mother and her young looking at their nest one last time. The elaborate and ritualized airborne gymnastics is their way of saying goodbye before they make their September flight to southern climes. There is an old German proverb that goes: *Zu Maria Geburt fliegen alle Schwalben furt.* [On Mary's birthday all the swallows fly away.]

Because this 8th of September is Our Lady's Birthday, I find myself trying to imagine something of the years she is supposed to have spent in the Temple. I cannot help thinking how intensely she must have longed for the coming of the Messiah. She would have been too humble even to imagine that she would be his mother. She would have been more than happy simply to plead for his arrival and to offer herself to God for that purpose.

I ask Our Lady to be with me as I long for God in my next hour of prayer. A young German seminarian, Andreas, is already in the oratory, kneeling on the floor. I kneel down too a little distance away. Mary's purity meant that she was totally fixed on God, completely absorbed by him, loving him, praising him, worshipping him without end. That is what loving God with all my heart and soul and strength must mean. I reflect a little on Mary's purity. I bow my head to the ground and worship God. With head still bowed, I find myself repeating the phrase "Lord Jesus, I long for you." I do not feel any intense burst of joy, neither do I feel sad. I am simply kneeling there on the floor, repeating this phrase, alternating between a profound bow and an upward glance where I fix my eyes on the tabernacle. Every so often I get distracted but each time the repeated phrase draws me back and helps me regain my focus.

Between our house and the river there is an untidy lawn which slopes almost imperceptibly downward for 30 yards until it reaches a tiny wall, beyond which is the water. This morning it is still sunny and warm. I walk down to the water and each time my feet touch the grass numerous tiny insects are released from the lawn like tiny drops of water spraying into the air. I sit on a green plastic chair at the bank of the river next to a giant weeping willow tree. Its long branches sway like a heavy curtain over the water and the lowest green leaves dance upon the river's surface. Across from me a fisherman's boat is moored near *Pfaueninsel*, his line disappearing below the water as he watches patiently.

Vitus, the portly and avuncular priest who is guiding me through this month of prayer, tells me there is a little chapel at the back of the infirmary. I decide to pray there in the afternoon. It is a small square room, with a low ceiling and walls painted white. The brown metal tabernacle is a modern design. A sphere is embedded in the centre and from it four tongues of flame stream out in the form of a cross. The tabernacle is set in the centre of a large stained glass window of subdued colours — chestnut, mauve and grey.

I bow down at the beginning in a gesture of adoring God. Vitus had suggested a different focus for prayer but I cannot get beyond adoration at the moment. That is where it feels right to be. I have always believed that the best way to pray is the way you pray best. I can hear a nurse talking to one of the old priests in the room next door. It sounds like a conversation they have had many times before: he does not understand what is going on and she repeatedly explains things to him with firm politeness. Through the open window I can hear two other elderly priests conversing together in the courtyard. One is obviously hard of hearing because the other has to say everything twice. And like the human background noise that accompanies my prayer, there is the continual flow of thoughts and distractions that come and go. I do not get upset about the distractions; I let them pass away and continue to focus my gaze on the tabernacle and my heart on adoring God. At times family and friends come to mind and I bring them before the Lord.

I decide to spend two hours in continual prayer rather than just one. I want to be generous in adoring God. I remember the many times I have spent two hours in other activities — chatting with friends, going to the cinema, travelling by car or train. I know that I cannot adore God adequately. But I also realize the saints are there to help me. So I borrow the Virgin Mary's utter adoration and offer that to God; I ask Mary Magdalene for her passionate adoration and give that to God too; I turn to Mary's husband Joseph and he loans me his adoration that never vacillated despite not living to see any of Jesus' miracles; I ask John the Beloved Disciple for his pure eyes to gaze at the Master.

In the second hour I develop a headache, possibly from staring at one point for so long. For a moment I feel discouraged at the thought that I am nothing. But then I say to God — "I am happy be a creature and I am glad you alone are the Creator. I thank you for creating me and I rejoice in the greatness of my soul which is in your image."

As the two hours draw to a close, I "baptize" some of the pop songs I like to sing, applying the lyrics to God. For instance I sing in my heart a few Beatles' numbers: "I want to hold your hand," "All my loving," and "From me to you."

I take out the rowing boat. It has turned chilly this afternoon. A damp wind seeps into me. As I leave our jetty a long rusty barge passes slowly by, and the smell of diesel from its loud engine fills my nostrils. My little boat is buffeted about in the waves created in its wake. The drone of the engine continues to sound as the barge makes its lazy way towards Potsdam and next to my boat this deep distant rumbling is balanced by the arpeggio of rippling water against the stern. Six black cormorants fly past in V formation, on their way back to the dead trees on the edge of *Pfaueninsel*. The metallic rhythm of someone hammering in a garden by the shore is carried across the water. A lone seagull calls out as it flies over the water and from the far side of the river a fellow seagull echoes its cry.

In the evening I return to the chapel. There is nobody there and I feel freer to express physically my worship and adoration of God by sitting on my heels with my knees touching the floor, my head against the carpet. This evening I am tired and it is more difficult to focus. I get distracted by other thoughts, but each time I become aware of the distractions I return to adoring God . . .

I wake up and the room is much darker than normal because there is no sun shining through the light curtains. Instead the gloom of autumn envelops everything. I hesitantly pull back the curtains and already feel subdued in the face of the dark grey sky that hangs motionlessly over the trees and the water. But then as I begin to shave, often a moment blessed with unexpected insights, I remember that I have begun the day by praying to God as well as Mary, my guardian angel and the saints. I have asked them to be with me and help me. Do I believe it? Do I believe that not only some of the best people who ever existed, but also the Creator of all is here with me? I pronounce a resounding "yes" as I guide the blade along my chin. And there is joy in my heart at this realization. Whatever the exterior weather may be like, God has made this day and has given me so much. The sun shines inside me.

My faith is simple. I do not dwell within a mystical cloud of unknowingness from which I can extract extraordinary nuggets of wisdom. My faith is no-frills and traditional; it is down to earth as a way of rising up to heaven. I am helped enormously by reading the Bible, receiving the body and blood of Jesus at mass, adoring him in the tabernacle, going to confession regularly, and saying the Rosary. These are the elementary blocks upon which my faith is built.

Certain Catholics dismiss some practices I hold dear as out-dated forms of superstition. I am not suggesting they ought to copy my devotions. The goal is God, and whatever good means brings you closest to your divine goal is best for you. I have met many older priests who as young seminarians were force-fed a strict diet of litanies and the public declaration of faults. They never recovered. One of my fellow retreatants has difficulties with Mary because an unhelpful brand of Marian piety was imposed on him as a young seminarian. I feel sorry for people who have been wounded in the name of religion, but it is not going to stop me apologizing for what I believe in.

It is not as if I have failed to explore other ways and traditions. When I first entered the Jesuits, I participated in a week-long workshop given by Tony de Mello, the Indian

Jesuit sage, shortly before his death. He was an excellent communicator, and managed to instruct us, entertain us, provoke us, and have us begging for more, despite talking for over five hours each day — without notes. I clearly remember the encouraging words he spoke to an elderly Jesuit brother at the workshop, a man who was at times bewildered by what was said, but who nevertheless sat there humbly and peacefully each day, his Rosary beads wrapped around his right hand. Tony glanced at him before turning to us all and announcing solemnly, "the Rosary is the highest form of contemplative prayer." That was Tony — an enigmatic and very private man, whose worst nightmare was to become anyone's guru, and who picked and sampled like a modern deejay from Buddhism, Hinduism, Hassidic tales, psychology, and Catholic spirituality to chisel out a uniquely stirring and provocative new groove.

As an impressionable seminarian I flirted briefly with Zen Buddhism, struck by the enthusiasm of certain Catholic priests who highlighted its compatibility with Christianity. But in the end I was too fascinated by Jesus to opt for a belief system that displays indifference to the question of whether God exists or not. I was drawn to Judaism in a more substantial way. After all, it was the culture and religion of Jesus, and I had the good fortune to meet several fine Jewish people who told me about their faith and way of life. But over the years I realized the revolutionary truth — I am sitting on a goldmine when it comes to my own faith. I have a heavenly bodyguard, my guardian angel, on duty 24/7. I am forgiven my sins by simply admitting them in the presence of a priest and telling God I am sorry I have offended him and want to change for the better. And where else would God humiliate himself to the extent of becoming nourishment for me, a divine food I can avail myself of daily? The riches I have at my disposal are unsurpassable. Why go looking for uncertain offerings somewhere else when I have inexhaustible wealth where I am?

The small chapel in our section of the house is empty again when I get there at 8.30 this morning. I spend most of the time on my knees, singing hymns of adoration in a low voice before the tabernacle. I bow my head to the floor repeatedly, and each time hold that position for a minute, then raise my head again. Like a Muslim prostrated on a prayer mat facing Mecca, I bow my forehead to the carpet as I face the tabernacle. The fervent Catholic and author of *The Lord of the Rings*, J.R.R. Tolkien, wrote to his son: "I put before you the one great thing to love on earth: the Blessed Sacrament . . . There you will find romance, glory, honor, fidelity, and the true way of all your loves upon earth, and more than that . . ."

The summer has not definitively abandoned us. Looking out the window of my room I see the bright yellow wall and charcoal-grey tiles at the gable end of our neighbour's house. The yellow is even more luminous with the sun shining upon it. Above the house the blue sky extends indefinitely, a few wispy white clouds hanging from it. I return to the infirmary chapel which is empty. As always I start by asking saints for help and then turn to the Holy Spirit. I kneel before God and adore him. Again I feel drawn to stay with adoration, rather than follow the program focused on salvation history that Vitus has given me. I anticipate telling Vitus tomorrow that God is drawing me one way and he is proposing an alternative route, and that I am beginning to feel strained in the middle because I am being tugged from both ends. And I plan to tell him gently that I am here to listen to God rather than him. But I realise these anxious thoughts are not from God. They bring me away from my focus now. I can leave my showdown meeting with Vitus until the morning. There is no need to rehearse it now. I return to adoring God, again borrowing from Mary her adoration, from John his pure gaze, from Mary of Magdalene her passionate longing, from Joseph his permanent worship. I prostrate my head regularly to the floor. My body needs to express the sense of worship and awe my soul feels.

I do not want to disregard Vitus' suggestion totally, so in the afternoon I decide to row out onto the lake and reflect on my own story of being loved by God through the events and people who have graced my life. Since I instinctively get into "adoration mode" in the chapel, the lake seems appropriate for this more reflective and autobiographical exercise. There is no wind today, just the gentlest murmur of a breeze. The lake is like a pulsing, vibrating mirror, subtle ripples racing continually across its glassy surface. I row out about hundred yards, pull the oars in, and begin to look back on my life. In the mirror of my mind myriad faces appear, of people who have nourished me with love. Events surface from the past, I look at them in gratitude, and then they float away, sinking back into the depths of memory.

I meet Vitus as usual at twenty past nine in the morning, immediately after my prayer in the chapel. I thank him for suggesting that I look at my salvation history yesterday. I tell him about my helpful marine meditation. However, I also express a sense of anxiety: adoring God is touching me in a deep way and I do not want to abandon this form of prayer. When I adore God in the chapel, I become aware of my own littleness, but in a non-threatening away. I see how inadequately I love God, I see how little I understand about him, I see how fragile my faith in him is and how tenuous my hope. And I tell Jesus how sorry I am that I do not love him more. But I also find that through dint of wanting to love him more and articulating these desires in his presence, a new space is opening up in my heart. It is as though the more I desire, the more the Lord enlarges the capacity of my heart to receive him. This gives me a deep peace and joy. And presumably the ultimate purpose of the pointers Vitus has given me is to lead to the very love and adoration that I am already practising! "That's fine," he replies with easy good humor.

In the afternoon, I am back in the domestic chapel which is once again empty. As usual I ask God for the grace to love him with all my heart, soul and strength. As I prostrate myself to the ground, I feel that I could gladly worship God like this for all eternity. Worship, awe, adoration and reverence are part of the language in which my love expresses itself to God. Each person has a different way of loving. And perhaps my soul's thirst to adore is one way of compensating for the excessively critical nature of my mind that tends to raise me up at others' expense. When I judge, I situate myself above others and look down; when I adore, I am happily at the bottom looking upwards. If I adored anything less than God, I would become a slave; but by adoring God, I enter freedom.

Often I meet Father Michael in the corridor as he laboriously pushes his Zimmer frame along. He looks at me

with coral-blue eyes and puts everything into his smile —
so moving it could break your heart.

As I go toward the chapel, I decide to pray with the
words of Mary's *Magnificat*. This outburst of praise and
adoration from Mary is like an aria that marks a joyously
reflective moment in an opera, a moment to savor as Mary
ponders on God's goodness towards herself and Israel. It is
a topsy-turvy song as well, for the meek, humble and poor
turn out to be the unexpected and real winners in history. A
fellow priest once suggested to me that Mary could never
possibly have said these verses or sung them, as the case
may be, since practically everything in the *Magnificat* can
be traced back to books of the Old Testament, such as the
First Book of Samuel, the Psalms, and Malachi. I agreed
with him that none of the verses was original, but for me
this fact led to a different conclusion. It was a heartening
reason for believing Mary uttered them. After all, she was
thoroughly conversant with the Scriptures, and like many
devout Jews, would have preferred to use God's own Word
to address her Lord, rather than words she made up, even
though her words would have been the most wonderful
human words imaginable.

But someone could counter that there was nobody there
to record Mary's words, which proves that the *Magnificat*
was made up much later. This argument does not convince
me. After all, why should anyone be surprised that Mary
clearly remembered these words that marked such a grace-
filled moment in her life? Indeed if they were the lyrics of
a song of praise, Mary would be even more likely to
remember them exactly. And even if she did not sing that
day, we know that her intelligence was luminous and

unstained, since she was preserved from original sin. So it does not stretch credulity to believe that this most intelligent of women had perfect recall and later would have been able to pass on her words verbatim to the Gospel author.

I bow in adoration before Jesus truly present in the tabernacle, and ask Mary, the only creature whose breath has such purifying power, to repeat the following words with me:

> My soul glorifies the Lord and my spirit rejoices in God my Savior, for he has been mindful of the humble state of his servant. From now on all generations will call me blessed, for the Mighty One has done great things for me — holy is his name. His mercy extends to those who fear him, from generation to generation. He has performed mighty deeds with his arm; he has scattered those who are proud in their inmost thoughts. He has brought down rulers from their thrones but has lifted up the humble. He has filled the hungry with good things but has sent the rich away empty. He has helped his servant Israel, remembering to be merciful to Abraham and his descendants forever, even as he said to our fathers.

Acknowledgements

What do you have that you did not receive?

St Paul, First Letter to the Corinthians 4:7

Best of all is it to preserve everything in a pure, still heart, and let there be for every pulse a thanksgiving, and for every breath a song.

Konrad von Gesner (1516-1565)

These words of Saint Paul from the First Letter to the Corinthians remind me that everything I have is a free gift of God. Not only is everything I have from God, but also all that I am. God drew me from absolute nothingness and gave me my very being. Before I was able to give him anything, he gave me so much. My thanks then go first of all and above all to the One who created and redeemed me.

I am also grateful for the example of so many people who have lived Christianity with ardent love and unflagging generosity, especially Mary, Maria, Joseph, John, Ignatius, Gabrielle, and Cecilia. They have set stupendous standards. I hope they spur me and many others to ascend to a higher plane, in order to be graced with the single-minded vision and total availability that characterize each of our guardian angels.

199

Bibliography

Da Ponte, Lorenzo. *Memoirs*, translated by Elisabeth Abbott, edited and annotated by Arthur Livingston, introduction by Charles Rosen. New York: New York Review of Books, 2000.

Ganss, George E. *Ignatius of Loyola: The Spiritual Exercises and Selected Works*. Classics of Western Spirituality series. Mahwah, N.J.: Paulist Press, 1991.

Gide, André. *La Symphonie Pastorale*. Paris: Éditions Gallimard, 1925.

Journet, Charles. *The Meaning of Evil*, translated by Michael Barry. London: Geoffrey Chapman, 1963.

Jouve, Pierre Jean. *Mozarts Don Giovanni*. Paris: Librairie Plon, édition revue, 1968.

Kierkegaard, Søren. *Either/Or Part I*, edited and translated with introduction and notes by Howard V. Hong and Edna H. Hong. Princeton, N.J.: Princeton University Press, 1987.

Maupassant, Guy de. *Claire de Lune*. Paris: Éditions Conard, 1909.

"Passio Sanctae Caeciliae" (anonymous), in *Sanctuarium seu Vitae Sanctorum*, edited by Boninus Mombritius. Paris: Monks of Solesmes, 1910, 2 volumes. The passion of Saint Cecilia is in Volume 1, pp. 332-341.

Mozart, Wolfgang Amadeus. *Mozart's Letters, Mozart's Life: selected letters*, edited and newly translated by Robert Spaethling. New York: W.W. Norton & Company, 2000.

Index

Other Books by Thomas Casey

Humble and Awake
Coping with Our Comatose Culture

The overlooked virtue of humility is presented as a cure to the coma that grips our culture. Casey draws on diverse sources—literature, film, philosophy, popular culture—to offer a readable and challenging, frequently moving, meditation on where we really are and what we need to do to awaken.

ISBN 978-0-87243-265-9   **Paperback**

208 pp   **$12.95**

Life and Soul
New Light on a Sublime Mystery

"With a fresh and spiritual voice, Fr. Tom Casey sets out the beauty, powers, and destiny of the human soul. He draws on the scriptures, philosophy, theology, art, literature and history to construct a timely and attractive masterpiece."

Gerald O'Collins, S.J.

ISBN 978-0-87243-267-3   **Paperback**

192 pp   **$16.95**